EVERYDAY ASTROLOGY

EVERYDAY ASTROLOGY

*A guide to understanding
your horoscope*

JILL DAVIES

CHANCELLOR
PRESS

First published in 1992 by Chancellor Press,
an imprint of Reed International Books Ltd.,
Michelin House, 81 Fulham Road,
London SW3 6RB

ISBN 1 85152 141 0

Printed in Hong Kong

TITLE PAGE:
Ptolemaic zodiac. After an early 16th century woodcut

CONTENTS

PART ONE

WHAT IS ASTROLOGY?

ASTROLOGY: THE SEARCH FOR A PATTERN

Since the dawn of time, Man has kept an unceasing watch on the skies, to try to determine a design in the Universe, and to understand its purpose. It is the correlation of those observations with events on Earth that has given birth to Astrology.

While we may not yet (if, indeed, ever) fully understand its purpose, at least we know there *is* a pattern. And astrologers believe that, in the same way that every single human cell is imprinted with the genetic code, every atom in the microcosm carries the pattern of the macrocosm. This concept is embodied in the phrase, 'As above, so below', and is at the heart of astrological belief.

We cannot make out the pattern on the atom, but we can look up to the skies, where the same design is repeated. Spread before us we can see the cosmic pattern in its entirety, and can better understand how our tiny contribution fits into the larger plan.

If you look at the small illustration opposite, you will see merely a confusing, seemingly random mass of coloured dots. But from a distance the beauty of the scene is revealed as Seurat's masterpiece of pointillism, and the whole design becomes clear. Astrology allows us to see, and to interpret, that overall pattern, and to develop our understanding of its meaning and relevance to ourselves.

An astrological Horoscope, or birth chart, is a symbolic representation of the Solar System and shows the precise planetary position at the moment you took your first independent breath. The great psychiatrist Carl Gustav Jung said, 'Whatever is born, or done, in this moment of time, takes on the qualities of this moment of time', and it is this simple statement that forms the basis of Astrology.

A Horoscope shows us which qualities you 'take on' at the moment of birth and can be likened to a road map. The map can show you alternative routes, warn you of hazards, suggest short cuts. But whether you drive recklessly or carefully, whether you use the information in your map or ignore it, is up to you. Most importantly, *the choice of direction is yours*.

Astrology is all about understanding. And to understand yourself is to understand more clearly your own *unique* place in the Universe. Since even the smallest atom reflects the grand design of Creation, to see yourself as an essential part of the rich and limitless Whole is a deep and fulfilling experience.

You may not be able to see what this is meant to be . . .

. . . but, if you stand back, the picture becomes clear

WHAT IS A HOROSCOPE ?

Many factors contribute to your character – genetic, environmental, socioeconomic and cultural – and to these we might usefully add 'astrological'. The nature of this astrological factor can be seen in your Horoscope.

Deriving from a hybrid mixture of Latin and Greek – *hora* ('time') and *skopos* ('observer') – the word 'Horoscope' therefore means an observation of the hour of birth and, as we have seen, a birth chart, or Horoscope, is a symbolic representation of the precise planetary position at the moment of birth.

To an astrologer, this Horoscope is a 'blueprint' of your *potential*. Hidden talents, predispositions of character, probable attitudes, vocational direction can be pinpointed with amazing accuracy.

From an architect's blueprint in the builder's hand, we can see the likely shape of a building and determine its purpose. If there is no provision for a kitchen, the building is unlikely to be a house. A tower and a belfry might indicate a church. A gymnasium and a laboratory could hold the promise of a school.

As with the architect's blueprint, so an astrological birth chart shows your likely 'shape' and purpose, or direction.

Are you likely to have a problem controlling your temper? How will you react emotionally? Will you communicate effectively, or will you find it difficult to put your point of view across? What sort of people will you find attractive? What is your ideal career?

The number of questions that a skilfully interpreted Horoscope can answer is practically unlimited. And in this book we hope to show – in simple terms – how you, too, can interpret your own *unique* Horoscope, and answer some of the questions about yourself that may have puzzled you, or lain unexplained, all your life.

From the cosmology of the Chaldeans, originating several thousand years before the birth of Christ, to the present day, Man has recorded the cycle of the Universe, linking the planetary pattern to events on Earth.
The original 'star-gazers' (astron – star) were skilled astronomers and, indeed, until the seventeenth century astrology and astronomy were the same science

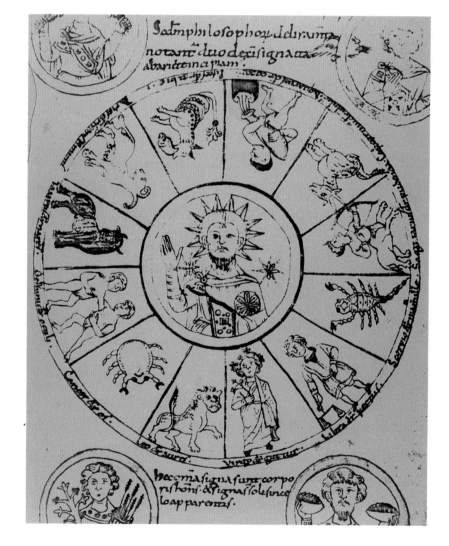

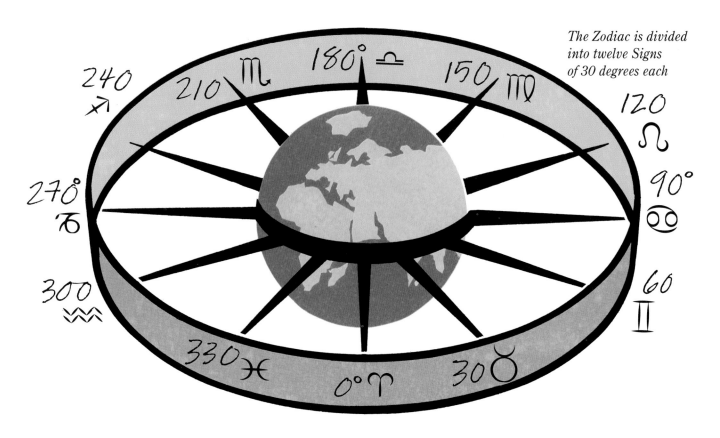

The Zodiac is divided into twelve Signs of 30 degrees each

PLANETS, SIGNS AND HOUSES: THE 'NUTS' AND 'BOLTS' OF ASTROLOGY

First of all, we must look at the basic tools of astrological interpretation – the factors that give us the information to work on.

Your Horoscope, or birth chart, will be drawn as a circle divided into twelve sections, each section representing a Sign of the Zodiac. (The word 'Zodiac' itself comes from the Greek word *xodiakos*, meaning a circle of animals.)

In *astronomical* terms the Zodiac is a band in the heavens extending to 8 degrees either side of the Ecliptic, which is another name for the *apparent* path of the Sun. We emphasize the word 'apparent' because, of course, the Sun does not follow a path round the Earth – the Earth revolves around the Sun. But Astrology is geocentric, which means we take the Earth (our viewpoint) as the centre of the Solar System, and imagine that the Planets revolve around *us*. On this 16-degree band (which we call the Zodiac) the Planets are disposed against an imaginary backdrop of the twelve Signs.

So an investigation into your Horoscope would initially examine the disposition of the Planets. What Signs are occupied by what Planets ?

Even if you know nothing else at all about astrology, you'll probably know your Sun Sign (what newspaper columnists call your 'Star Sign') – the month-long period during which the Sun is moving through your birth Sign. But to say that you're a Virgo or a Gemini is, like

the tip of an iceberg, only one-tenth of the picture.

For there are ten celestial bodies (for astrological convenience called 'Planets') in everybody's chart, and each Planet 'looks after' a particular facet of your chacacter. When we look at the disposition of these Planets, and at the angular relationship they make with each other, we can begin to see a pattern emerging, a pattern which is unique to *you*.

A birth chart is multi-layered. The basic layer will show the disposition of the Planets, and how they are influenced by the nature, or character, of the Signs in which they fall. A second layer of your Horoscope will show the aspects, or relationships, made by the ten Planets in your chart between each other. Some of these aspects will be stressful or challenging; some will be helpful or harmonious. All will combine to make you the individual you undoubtedly are. In the third layer (on which we will be concentrating in this book), we can look at those same Planets to see which Houses they fall into.

Not only is your Horoscope divided into twelve Signs – Aries, Taurus, Gemini, Cancer, and so on – it is overlaid by a further division into twelve Houses, or areas of life; compartments of experience, which show us where the energies of each Planet are expressed.

Now, whilst you may share your birthday with many millions of people worldwide, it is highly unlikely that you will share your Horoscope with any of them. You may even know someone born the same day as you but – unless he or she is born at the same location, and at the same moment – your Horoscope will be as *unique* as

you yourself are. *For the moment (and location) of birth gives us the Ascendant, or Rising Degree, and this is the key to a personal and highly individual document – your Horoscope.*

Later, in Part Two, we'll examine the importance of determining your Ascendant, and we'll show you how to identify the planetary pattern within the Houses of your Horoscope, but first – back to basics!

THE SOLAR SYSTEM

There are ten celestial bodies in our Solar System: the Sun, the Moon, Mercury, Venus, Mars, Jupiter, Saturn, Uranus, Neptune and Pluto. All but the last three were known to the ancients, and are visible to the naked eye. Each Planet has 'rulership' over one or more Signs, and 'flavours' its Sign or Signs accordingly.

Before 1781, when Uranus was discovered, there were only seven known Planets ruling twelve Signs. Mars ruled both Aries and Scorpio; Jupiter influenced Sagittarius and Pisces; Saturn held dominion over Capricorn and Aquarius and so on. However, when Pluto – the outermost Planet – became known in 1930, rulership of the Signs was apportioned as we know it today:

The Sun rules the Sign of Leo
The Moon rules the Sign of Cancer
Mercury rules the Signs of Gemini and Virgo
Venus rules the Signs of Taurus and Libra
Mars rules the Sign of Aries
Jupiter rules the Sign of Sagittarius
Saturn rules the Sign of Capricorn
Uranus rules the Sign of Aquarius
Neptune rules the Sign of Pisces
Pluto rules the Sign of Scorpio

Above: Division of a Horoscope by Sign

Top right: The planetary rulerships prior to 1781

Bottom right: The planetary rulerships since 1930

ELEMENTS

Each Sign belongs to one of the four Elements: Fire, Earth, Air and Water. These correspond to Intuition, Sensation, Thinking and Feeling respectively, and represent the nature of the Sign.

Aries, Leo and Sagittarius belong to the Fire Element; Taurus, Virgo and Capricorn are Earth; Gemini, Libra and Aquarius make up the Air triplicity; and Cancer, Scorpio and Pisces are Water.

The Fire Signs (Aries, Leo and Sagittarius) are very quick to grasp a situation, and tend to act in an instinctive way. They inspire other, less volatile, Signs, and are confident and outgoing, warm-hearted and generous in spirit.

Earth Signs (Taurus, Virgo and Capricorn) are more factual. They deal in tangibles, rather than concepts, and are the most practical of the Signs. They see Life in straightforward, material terms and are loyal, resistant and constant.

Air is an Element of interchange, circulation and connection, and this is how the Air Signs (Gemini, Libra and Aquarius) operate. Cerebral, detached and impersonal, they subject everything to their reason, logic and cool rationale.

Powerful and deep, like their Element, the Water Signs (Cancer, Scorpio and Pisces) are the Signs most 'in tune' with the subconscious, and respond on a feeling level. Compassionate and imaginative, they are extremely sensitive and emotional.

MODES

The Signs are further subdivided into Modes: Cardinal, Fixed and Mutable. The word 'Mode' when applied to a Sign means its style of operating.

The Modes are often referred to as 'Quadruplicities', for there are four Signs – one of each Element – in each Mode.

The Cardinal Signs – Aries, Cancer, Libra and Capricorn – are the initiators of action. Eager, and impatient of delay, they are the ones who forge ahead with alacrity. They like to be in charge; 'Number One'. If you're born

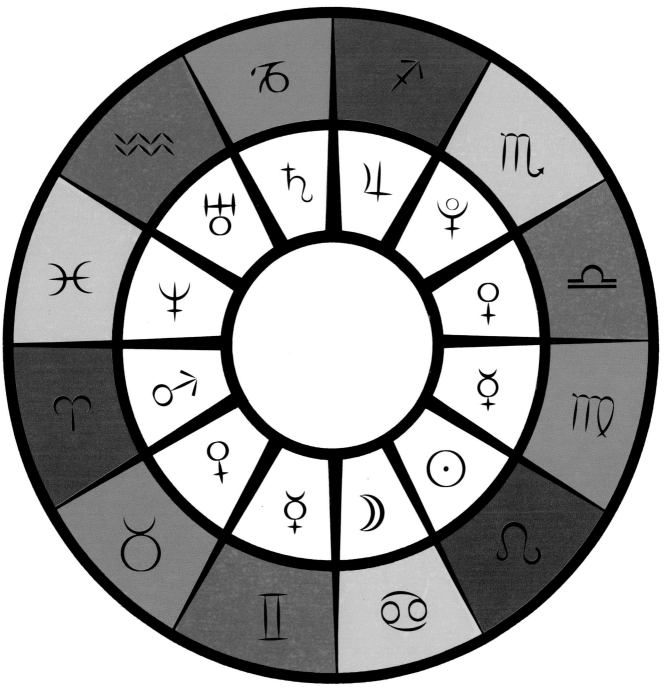

under a Cardinal Sign, you are the type of person who has the initial spark, the forceful feelings, the bright ideas, the ambition and drive. 'Say, this is a great old barn – why don't we put on the show here?' says the Cardinal Sign, his eyes lighting up and shining with enthusiasm.

Taurus, Leo, Scorpio and Aquarius are Fixed Signs, and their role in the Zodiac is to have a stabilizing and actualizing influence. The Fixed Signs have staying power, and take the quickly discarded 'bright ideas' (the Cardinal Signs soon lose their initial impetus) and *make them work*. 'It may well be a great old barn,' says the Fixed Sign, 'but we'll have to fix the hole in the roof, and make some provision for car parking. I'll set up a Task Force.'

Mutable Signs – Gemini, Virgo, Sagittarius and Pisces – have a flexible, adapting influence. They can 'roll with the punches' and are happy to negotiate with others to achieve the desired end result. Ever willing to compromise, their motto is 'Anything for a quiet life'. The Mutable Signs are generally easy-going sort of people, taking what Life throws at them, and changing to suit the circumstances. 'If putting on a show in the old barn is going to be a problem,' says the Mutable Sign, 'why don't we cut our losses and hold a jumble sale in the village hall instead?'

POLARITIES

The Signs are further subdivided into Polarities: Positive (Masculine) and Negative (Feminine).

The Polarities do not imply any sexual nature or predisposition, but correspond more to objectivity and Yang (Positive) and subjectivity and Yin (Negative).

The Fire and Air Signs are Positive; the Water and Earth Signs are Negative.

Each Sign, therefore, is unique and unreplicated in nature or character or style by any other Sign.

THE PLANETS

For the purposes of Astrology, the Sun and Moon – more accurately named 'the Luminaries' or 'the Lights' – are included in the ten Planets which make up our Solar System.

In a birth chart, each of these Planets symbolically represents a psychological function – a facet of your personality – and the position of each Planet by Sign and House gives a very strong indication of your likely traits and characteristics.

☉ The **Sun** signifies your sense of identity, your will, self-image, and how you want to be seen by the outside world. It is your personal powerhouse, the core of your personality, and the single most important planet in your birth chart.

The style of your individuality is shown by the placement of the Sun, and it describes your ultimate destiny, your purpose in life; your goal. The Sun is the ruler of the Sign of Leo and the House of your Horoscope with Leo on its cusp.

☽ The **Moon** has no light of its own, but reflects the light of the Sun. And it is this reflective quality that is shown by the position of the Moon in your Horoscope. For what is reflected are the instinctive responses you learned in childhood, and deeply engrained patterns of behaviour. It has been said that if the Sun represents the goal or destination you *will* to reach, then the Moon is the path you are *obliged* to take because of the constraints of your instinctive reactions.

The Moon describes your early years and the relationship you had with your mother (or nurturing parent), as well as the way in which you will nurture in return. It rules your emotions. It shows your needs, and how you respond to the needs of others. The Moon rules the Sign of Cancer, and the House of your Horoscope with Cancer on its cusp.

☿ Mentality, speech and thought patterns are governed by **Mercury**. This Planet shows how you make connections and relationships, and how you communicate. Unlike Jupiter, which represents your faith and beliefs, Mercury has no in-built bias, nor is it concerned with principles or ethics. Mercury is completely amoral and deals solely in rationale and concepts. It can be likened to the postman who is responsible neither for writing the letters he handles, nor for the reactions they engender: Mercury simply operates as a neutral medium for the interchange of information. Mercury rules the Signs of Gemini and Virgo and the Houses of your Horoscope with those Signs on the cusps.

♀ The softer side of your personality is shown by the placement of **Venus** in your chart. In fact, Venus tends to 'soften' everything it touches in your chart. Amongst other things, it bestows your sense of aesthetic appreciation, your 'taste'. Venus is the planetary symbol of harmony, co-operation, giving, the need to 'relate' and loving feelings. It represents what you find attractive in others and how you seek to attract; what you want from relationships and what you have to give in return. Venus also symbolizes what you value; your value system. Everything which is pleasing and pleasurable is the province of this lovely Planet, sometimes called 'the lesser benefic'. Venus rules the Signs of Taurus and Libra and the Houses of your Horoscope with those Signs on the cusps.

↗Resourceful and competitive **Mars** shows your ♂ drive, how you use your energies and how you assert yourself. Termed by the ancients 'the lesser malefic', Mars shows the ruthless side of your nature – how you go about getting what you want, how you fight for what you hold dear.

Mars is the astrological adrenalin which fuels your combative spirit, and makes you want to be 'the firstest with the mostest'. It makes for courage, resourcefulness and positivity. Most of all, it shows the quality of your *aggression* (however its expression is modified by the nature of the Sign into which it falls). Mars, in short, represents the driving force that impels you to survive. Mars rules the Sign of Aries, and the House of your Horoscope with Aries on its cusp.

♃ Wherever we find **Jupiter** ('the greater benefic') in a birth chart, we find confidence, faith and vision. Buoyantly optimistic, Jupiter's function is to exaggerate all it touches. Big is beautiful, to Jupiter's way of thinking! However, it inflates and expands quite indiscriminately – bad points are made worse and good points are made better.

Whereas Mercury is concerned with mentality in what might be described as a 'sterile' environment – thought for thought's sake – Jupiter gives you the ability to think ahead, to understand the ramifications of your thought processes, to appreciate long-term significance and purpose. With Jupiter you can find *meaning*. And Jupiter in a birth chart also shows the nature of your belief system – what you find meaningful – and the measure of your faith. Of course, this may not necessarily mean religious or political faith, but we all uphold some sort of creed or moral standard, or set of principles. Jupiter is very strongly associated with principles, and matters on a higher plane than the strictly mundane. Jupiter's inflationary nature widens your horizons and allows you to see the 'big picture'. And a mixture of thought with 'vision' (seasoned with principles) leads to Jupiter's greatest gift: wisdom.

Jupiter rules the Sign of Sagittarius and the House of your Horoscope with Sagittarius on the cusp.

♄ A perfect counter-balance to Jupiter's expansive nature is the restrictive function of 'the greater malefic': **Saturn**. Saturn's purpose is to control, to define and to limit. It creates a need for order and security. The Planet is sometimes known as 'the Great Teacher', and Saturn's lessons are often uncomfortable, particularly in youth. (Mastering your Saturn may not be possible until the second half of life.) Saturn obliges you to 'learn the hard way', through denial and delay; to face up to responsibilities, duties and obligations, and to accept discipline and restriction.

Also known as 'the Cosmic Taskmaster', this Planet offers no easy options in confronting Saturnian issues, and is therefore often associated with pain. And, hand in glove with pain, goes fear. But Saturn's nature is not wholly negative, for nothing in Astrology is one-sided: the positive side to Saturn is that discipline and effort produce results and slow but steady realistic progress. Saturn rules the Sign of Capricorn and the House of your Horoscope with Capricorn on the cusp.

The outer Planets – Uranus, Neptune and Pluto – operate as a trinity to transform, dissolve and renew. However, because of the length of their orbits and the consequently long time they take to travel through each Sign, their influence is considered to be generational rather than personal.

♅ Freedom, originality and independence are expressed by the Planet **Uranus**. Uranus represents revolution, unorthodoxy, rebellion and deviation from the norm. Whatever this Planet touches in your chart it will excite, agitate and shock, for it represents the desire for change and innovation. Uranus rules the Sign of Aquarius and the House of your Horoscope with Aquarius on the cusp.

♆ Whereas hard, cold Saturn is driven to crystallize and define, nebulous **Neptune** dissolves and disseminates. It knows no boundaries and transcends mundane limitations. Neptune has a refining and purifying quality, and wants to make perfect and render into an idealistic state whatever it contacts in your birth chart. However, a by-product of Neptune's wish for idealism is a lack (or blurring) of reality, deception, a tendency to see issues through rose-tinted spectacles. Used in its most positive sense, though, this Neptunian unacceptance of limitations can make possible the achievement and fulfilment of dreams and a transcendence (or escape from) the ordinary.

Neptune rules the Sign of Pisces and the House of your Horoscope with Pisces on the cusp.

♇ The furthermost and most recently known Planet in our Solar System is **Pluto**. Its function in your chart is to bring about change in a transformative way, by destroying the old order and giving birth to the new. Pluto is like an astrological compost-heap: breaking down still-living matter and transforming it into a different medium, from which will come new life and renewed hope.

Accepting the need for endings and transmutation can be frightening, for it requires relinquishment of the familiar with no promise of direct replacement in a known form. But the caterpillar that resists the evolutionary process of becoming a butterfly dies in the cocoon; yet the snake that accepts the painful necessity of sloughing off its old and outgrown skin emerges as a more beautiful, and ultimately more powerful, creature. Pluto rules the Sign of Scorpio and the House of your Horoscope with Scorpio on the cusp.

THE SIGNS OF THE ZODIAC

ARIES

TAURUS

GEMINI

LIBRA

SCORPIO

SAGITTARIUS

The astrological year begins with Aries, and the moment for the beginning of that Sign each year is astronomically determined. The point at which the Ecliptic (the apparent path of the Sun) intersects with the Equator, on the Sun's annual journey north, is known as the Vernal Equinox, or the first day of Spring, and it is astrologically designated 0° degrees Aries.

CANCER

LEO

VIRGO

CAPRICORN

AQUARIUS

PISCES

♈ ARIES

Positive · Cardinal Fire · Symbolized by The Ram

*The First Sign of the Zodiac, Aries is very like a new-
born baby – unsubtle, demanding and frequently loud!
The comparison is not meant to be a cruel one.
In the same way that an infant is a bundle of raw,
unshaped energies, Aries is a Sign of great simplicity,
and, like the baby, his motto is 'Me first'.*

H‌E IS COMPLETELY SELF-CENTRED. This should not be confused with selfishness, but Aries considers himself to be at the core of his personal universe and cannot comprehend the notion that he himself could possibly be positioned on the outer edges of anyone else's. And, like the baby around whom the entire household revolves, Aries takes it for granted that everyone else will dance attendance upon him, and gratify his needs.

But this life-long demand for attention springs not from arrogance nor, indeed, from an inflated sense of self-worth. It comes from a form of naivety. Aries does not understand that he may have to 'wait his turn' or that there may be other considerations to take into account. He sees Life in terms solely of his own boundaries, his own requirements, and, quite naturally, expects them to be met first.

Aries is fresh and direct, and completely guileless. He functions on very simplistic levels – black is black and white is white – and is bewildered when he first finds out that the rest of the world rarely behaves in the same way.

Aries is an exceedingly assertive Sign. Fired by Mars, he is motivated to be Number One. He's a leader, a go-getter, and he knows where he's going: straight ahead. Unfortunately, he can often ride rough-shod over others in his urge to get there. Aries is always in a hurry, and rarely stops to think out his plan before acting. Impatience is his middle name.

There isn't a malicious bone in his body. (When he offends, he does so unwittingly.) He is quick to anger, and even quicker to forget: Aries harbours neither spite nor a grudge. He's honest, direct, open, and fiercely loyal. He will defend his loved ones – and his principles – to the death, and he is unflinchingly courageous, unafraid to stand alone in the face of unilateral opposition.

Aries is not a team player. He's a natural pioneer, a loner, a maverick who has to carve his own way through life. He will not compromise his ideals for the sake of courting popularity, and his actions are clean-cut and above board. This is positively the last Sign to indulge in secretive machinations or dubious ethics. Aries nails his colours to the mast for all to see. He may fail, but he always goes down fighting, and he's rarely defeated in spirit.

In love he's surprisingly chivalrous. He has an idealistic view of romance, and fidelity comes high on his list of priorities.

His burning desire is to be 'special'. Whilst Capricorn strives to reach the top, the Ram is only interested in getting to the front. With his inability to be daunted, and his refusal to be gainsaid, he frequently achieves this.

♉ TAURUS

Negative · Fixed Earth · Symbolized by The Bull

*With quiet determination, Taurus, the Second Sign of
the Zodiac, plods patiently through life in a steadfast,
deliberate manner. She's the 'builder' of the Zodiac,
the one who takes the fanciful schemes and
ideas of her less-grounded Zodiacal brothers and sisters
and makes them work. She achieves this by the simplest
of methods: sheer hard graft.*

TAURUS KNOWS THERE ARE NO EASY OPTIONS. 'Soonest started; soonest finished', is her motto. She can be relied upon to put 100 per cent effort into all that she does, and it's a very rare Bull who will abandon a project halfway through. She has great staying power, seeing a job through to the end, no matter how arduous.

Taurus is eminently practical, in thought as well as deed. Her thinking is 'down to earth', and she calls a spade a spade, not an 'agricultural digging implement'. There is no nonsense about Taurus: she says what she means, and means what she says, and she's convinced that if everyone behaved the same way, life would be a lot easier all round.

The gimcrack and the cheap and shoddy hold no attraction for Taurus, who has an outstandingly strong sense of values. She believes in value for money, and she's prepared to pay for the best. And if she can't afford the best, she'll 'go without' until she can. Material security is important to her. She deals in tangibles, not pie-in-the-sky, however glamorous the prospect.

Taurus has little time for the poseur or the dilettante, weeding out such useless elements from her life with her in-built bullshit-detector. In their place she cultivates people who are as straightforward, decent and honest as she is, and no friend could be stauncher or more loyal than the Bull. When she commits herself to a friendship, it's for life, through thick and thin.

Although it may seem that there are few frills about Taurus, she is, in fact, extremely sensuous. Ruled by Venus, the Planet which is concerned with what is pleasurable, Taurus has an enhanced sense of beauty and a fine appreciation of what is pleasing to the senses.

In love, her ruling Planet Venus and her element, Earth, form a rich mix of earthy sensuality, and there's very little the Bull doesn't know about physical satisfaction and romantic pleasure.

Taurus adores luxury and all that is good and comfortable about life. Her artistic tastes are highly developed, and she may be musically talented. (Many Bulls are gifted singers for, physiologically, Taurus rules the throat. But, irrespective of whether it's La Scala or simply scales in the bathroom, most Bulls have melodic voices.)

An unwarranted reputation for obstinacy comes from the combination of Earth and the Fixed nature of the Sign, and this fixity applies equally to the Bull's opinions as to her actions. Often interpreted as 'stubbornness' and regarded as a character flaw by those who do not share the Bull's capacity for endurance, the Second Sign is gifted with an unyielding strength.

♊
GEMINI

Positive · Mutable Air · Symbolized by The Heavenly Twins

Gemini is the Third Sign of the Zodiac, and the combination of Air and Mutability makes him one of the most difficult Signs to pin down.

THE MOST VERSATILE MEMBER OF THE ZODIAC, Gemini lacks staying power. His boredom threshold is extremely low. He is constantly on the lookout for new experiences and stimulation, and he'll try anything once. He's the original 'Jack of all trades, master of none'.

He's highly intelligent, but rarely profound. Although he may appear to take only a superficial interest in what's going on around him, his agile brain will have skimmed off the salient points from the subject in hand and, to Gemini, the salient points are all that matter. Despite (or perhaps because of) this, he's capable of displaying amazing insight, forcing others to suspect they may have been underestimating him all along.

Gemini is the most quick-witted Sign of the Zodiac. Perceptive and bright (and impatient of slower-thinking folk) he'll rarely give his full attention to anyone or anything. This does not imply lack of interest on Gemini's part, however: it's simply that he's capable of thinking about several things at once.

Physically, Gemini retains his youthful good looks well into old age. There's something of the eternal child about him. His restless lifestyle ensures his metabolism is high, and accounts for his slim, athletic build. Gemini is rarely found slumped on the sofa watching TV, for he finds it difficult to relax. Everything is carried out at top speed: he talks faster, moves more quickly and uses his hands more than anyone else.

His telephone bill is usually enormous, for Gemini is the communicator of the Zodiac and is never happier than when gathering and exchanging information. His almost unquenchable thirst for knowledge means he's a veritable storehouse of facts and figures and titbits of gossip; and Mercury's influence means that he's impelled to pass them on.

Gemini is associated with the making of connections, with linking people together within relationships. His own relationships are likely to be made most easily with those with whom he has an intellectual rapport. Like his Element, Air, he prefers to keep his relationships light, friendly, and on the surface. He's an immensely sociable creature. His circle of friends is large and wide-ranging and he knows how to adapt himself in order to fit into any social context.

In love he likes to remain uncommitted. He may even 'play the field' well into middle age, for he's emotionally inconsistent. And he's likely to be a tremendous flirt.

Gemini is enthusiastic, optimistic, and full of crackling energy. He exudes charm, and can be devastatingly witty. He's friendly and – aptly, since he's represented by The Twins – twice as much fun as anyone else.

⊛ CANCER

Negative · Cardinal Water · Symbolized by The Crab

*So often dismissed as 'moody, shy and weepy',
the Fourth Sign of the Zodiac – Cancer – is, in fact, a
force to be reckoned with.*

THE WORD 'FORCE' IS CAREFULLY CHOSEN. Cancer is a Cardinal Sign, and cardinality implies drive, initiative, and impetus. Water is a powerful body and, when allied with impetus, it becomes the most dangerous medium there can be. For water quenches fire, combines with air in typhoons, sweeps away earth in landslides. An excess of water will burst river banks and cause tidal waves.

Cancer should not, therefore, be underestimated. Her 'shyness' is not timidity, but a cloak for her feelings; a protection against emotional exposure. Any tendency towards lachrymosity is prompted by her soft heart and excessive sensitivity, for Cancer is the most empathetic Sign of them all. Ruled by the Moon, her frequent changes of mood are caused by that Planet's rapid passage each month through all twelve Signs of the Zodiac, colouring her responses, emotions and instincts in twelve different way.

Underneath her protective shell is a kind and caring nature and yet – at the very heart of Cancer – there's a rock-hard nugget of determination and a generous measure of self-interest.

This determination, fuelled by her forceful cardinality, won't allow her to take a backseat in life. She'll surge ahead, like a tidal wave, sweeping everything before her. Water is hard to contain and will always find a way of going where it wants to.

And Cancer's 'self-interest' also means the interests of the 'family', her loved ones. She is driven by the need to nurture and protect those dear to her, and will defend them as thoroughly as she protects herself – fighting to the death, if need be. She's a gentle bully, chivvying and worrying (and sometimes snapping) out of loving concern.

Highly imaginative, Cancer is often surprisingly creative and artistic. She may also be gifted with the happy knack of making money, and the even happier facility of hanging on to it.

Money isn't the only thing that Cancer hangs on to. She finds it hard to relinquish anything, and carries round with her, all her life, old memories, old friends, old hurts and wounds, old friends, and old lovers. Even old tennis shoes. (They might come in handy one day, you see.) She takes comfort from her possessions, and the security of her surroundings.

In love she may mask her feelings, fearing rejection, afraid to trust. She's emotionally vulnerable. But once Cancer feels secure in a relationship, her love is deep and generous and intensely loyal. She loves to be cherished and comforted; and she loves to cherish and comfort in return. Nobody cuddles like a Cancer.

♌ LEO

Positive · Fixed Fire · Symbolized by The Lion

Like his jungle counterpart in the animal world,
Leo – the Fifth Sign – really is the
King of the Zodiac.

IN THE SAME WAY THAT LEO'S RULER, the Sun, overpowers all other lights, the magnitude (and magnificence) of Leo's personality blazes out as he stands, centre stage on whatever platform he chooses to occupy in Life.

There's nothing modest about Leo: he's a very efficient self-publicity machine. He likes to be appreciated for his efforts (and his uniqueness), and he derives pleasure from his magnanimity. His capacity for enjoyment is unaffected by the trials and tribulations of everyday living, and his zest for life seems to be unequalled by any other Sign.

He's an extremely proud creature and has many qualities in which he can justly take pride: he's generous of spirit, affectionate, charismatic and creative. But pride is also his downfall. Leo finds it almost impossible to admit he might be in the wrong, and pride combined with the Fixed nature of his Sign can result in bloody-mindedness and obstinacy.

His 'Achilles heel' is vanity. His craving to stand permanently under the spotlight, and his constant need for admiration, can attract sycophantic flattery – and, blinded by conceit, he's easily manipulated by the unscrupulous.

But allowances should be made for the Lion. If he's a 'show-off', it's because he's been the centre of attention all his life; and if he's cocky and conceited, it's because he's multi-talented, and can actually back up his boastful claims. If he's bossy, it's because he's the best person to wear the 'I'm in charge' badge.

Have no doubt about it: Leo is the best person to be in charge. He blends the staying-power of his Mode (Leo's a Fixed Sign) with the energy of his Element (Fire), to produce the steady banked-up heat of a boilerhouse furnace. With this, plus charisma, charm and a leonine touch of arrogance, the Lion can – and frequently does – move mountains. But he needs an audience and generous helpings of praise.

When it comes to romance, Leo's written the book. His tender (and skilful) love-making will leave his partner starry-eyed, and feeling cherished and adored. Leo is deeply sentimental, generously affectionate, warmly loving. But he's prone to jealousy (he must come first in his loved one's affections), and has a tendency to possessiveness.

Love him, or loathe him, there's no overlooking the Fifth Sign. Roaring Lion or purring pussycat, his mission in life is to make his mark with style and panache, and this the majestic, magnificent Lion rarely fails to do.

♍ VIRGO

Negative · Mutable Earth · Symbolized by The Virgin

*Mutability and the Earth Element combine in the adaptable
and practical Sixth Sign – Virgo.
Although Virgo and Gemini share the same ruler
(Mercury), the Planet manifests its characteristics in two
different ways. In Gemini, Mercury wants to link together
and to make connections, but in Virgo, the same Planet
wants to dissect, discriminate and analyse.*

VIRGO IS PRECISE AND METHODICAL IN HER THOUGHTS as well as in her actions, for her Element (Earth) adds a strong dose of practicality to Mercury's intellectual attributes. The Sixth Sign of the Zodiac is associated with service and duty, and Virgo is very strongly imbued with the work ethic. She sees duty and obligation as inescapable, and seeks to discharge her duty in practical ways.

She's the 'detail person', a perfectionist who's doomed by virtue of her exceedingly high standards to be perpetually disappointed. Very little in life comes up to Virgo's standards. The disappointment extends to herself, for she's her own severest critic. And even though she knows perfection is rarely obtainable, this is of little comfort to her, for it doesn't make second-best any more acceptable, as far as she's concerned.

Her dissatisfaction can often turn inwards and sour into neurosis, making her cranky and 'picky'. Highly strung, she needs order and method to act as a counterbalance for nervous tension. Work is an excellent channel for her nervous energies and enables her to validate her sense of 'self' through service. Virgo makes an ideal employee, for she finds it difficult to delegate and prefers to oversee each part of the operation herself. Her main fault lies in her obsession with analysing everything to death: she'll pick a thing to pieces in order to see how it works.

Virgo is often misrepresented as emotionally or physically frigid. The truth of the matter is that she is particularly discriminating and fastidious and this – combined with her inh rent modesty and shyness – has led to the universally accr (if not totally correct) interpretation of this facet of her ality. Yet there's a grain of truth in this generally held Virgo may often experience difficulties in her l ships. For although Virgo is of the lusty Earth ruled by airy Mercury, who restrains her e cool detachment and calm rationale.

This may result in an inhibition (or ' that Virgo approaches her intimate they were not so much matters of ' cises. She brings a kind of crisp and she's likely to compensate tive passion with pyrotechr'

Quiet, contained and 29 dependable person wh cal ways. She's kind and fortunate. She may shun t bold type on the credit list.

♎

LIBRA

Positive · Cardinal Air · Symbolized by The Scales

*Libra is the Seventh Sign,
and marks the beginning of the
second half of the Zodiac.*

CONTRARY TO POPULAR OPINION, and despite the fact that his glyph, or symbol, is the Scales, Libra is rarely well balanced! In fact, he's quite the opposite. His mood and opinion will swing first one way, then the opposite until, in time, a balanced result is obtained. The process of striving for balance can be long, for Libra – a Cardinal Air Sign – has actively to explore all the options, consider all the possibilities, before making a decision.

His god is logic. He subjects everything in life to his reasoning processes; discounting feelings and mistrusting intuition, relying only on rationale. No other considerations apply.

But Libra is not a coldly calculating robot. He's ruled by Venus, whose gentle and softening nature spurs him to relate and reconcile. Libra's glyph also suggests a bridge – a symbol of linkage.

Linking together can also be achieved by words, and Libra is the tactful diplomat of the Zodiac. He knows the value of compromise and achieves more through gentle persuasion than the more overt tactics of his fellow Cardinal Signs – Capricorn, Aries and Cancer. He is skilled at weighing and assessing the pros and cons of a situation in order to reach a fair result, a judicious verdict.

Libra's glyph, the Scales, signifies balance and equality, and Libra represents the drive to seek balance through the equalizing medium of a partner.

Sociable Venus seeks to harmonize, and unify, and this is translated into romantic attraction. Whereas Gemini is concerned with making connections, Libra has a very strong need to form relationships, to give and to receive loving affection, and to 'relate' to another. Through a partner, Libra is in some way able to 'validate' himself, and better express his sense of 'self'.

Libra cannot bear to be 'at odds' with anyone. His need for popularity and the constant approbation of others is paramount, and there is little he would not do in order to safeguard it.

His desire is to secure peace and harmony at all costs, for he cannot bear discord, the ugliness of confrontation or the responsibility of causing pain, and he is perfectly prepared to compromise his ideals in the pursuit of this. With the charm and good nature bestowed upon him by Venus, he rarely fails to reach his goal.

♏
SCORPIO

Negative · Fixed Water · Symbolized by The Scorpion

*Ruled by Pluto, god of the Underworld (Hades), and of
the Water Element, Scorpio is a Sign of great intensity
and power, and immense depth.*

REGENERATIVE IS THE WORD that best describes Scorpio's nature. For the Eighth Sign is also symbolized by the Phoenix, the mythological bird that rises from the ashes of its own destruction – its funeral pyre – to live again, to take on life in another form; to experience another cycle of being.

For Scorpio is concerned with endings of cycles and new beginnings; with death and resurrection; with renewal; with transformation.

Much of Scorpio's nature is hidden from us, and her motives are shrouded in secrecy. To the Eighth Sign, knowledge is power. For this reason she will not reveal too much for fear that others may gain the upper hand and attempt to manipulate her. Scorpio has a fundamental need to stay in control.

There is nothing shallow or wishy-washy about Scorpio. Her will-power is phenomenal and she is extremely purposeful. The force of her personality is such that it can suck your energy from you, leaving you drained, or it can inspire you to unscaled heights. Experience of Scorpio will not leave you unchanged.

In relationships she is as intense as everything else in her life. A Water Sign, her emotions run deep. Her need to control at all times may manifest itself as unreasonable possessiveness, and she can be extremely jealous.

Her memory is long. She will forget neither a kindness nor an injury. A Fixed Sign, she has staying power, and can wait (if need be) to the end of her lifetime in order to exact revenge. Cross her at your peril!

Scorpio has the ability to inspire fear or awe in others, because of the overwhelming force of her personality. But 'forcefulness' does not mean 'hardness' for, beneath the surface, lies a rich (if mainly untapped) vein of compassion. However, Scorpio prefers to help those who at least try to help themselves – so strong herself, she despises weakness.

Scorpio cannot live on a superficial level, and has to subject everything in life to the most thorough investigative scrutiny. For this reason, she excels at detection. (Because of Scorpio's association with 'death', forensic detection in particular is an ideal occupation for her, as is anything to do with the occult, which means 'hidden' or 'secret' – words which correspond to the nature of the Eighth Sign.)

But the word most associated with Scorpio is 'passion'. She can do nothing by half measures; she is all or nothing. She's a staunch and loyal friend, a tireless worker, a demanding lover, an implacable enemy.

Despite appearances (and reputation!) Scorpio is not the 'baddy' of the Zodiac. Like the Phoenix who rises from the ashes of its mortality to seek perfection in another form, Scorpio is compelled by Pluto to evolve ever onwards and ever upwards.

SAGITTARIUS

Positive · Mutable Fire · Symbolized by The Archer

*Sagittarius – the Ninth Sign –
is the unfettered, freedom-loving
gipsy of the Zodiac.*

His RESTLESS SPIRIT IS HARD TO CONTAIN. He's ruled by ebullient Jupiter, a Planet whose nature is characterized by the quality of growth and exaggeration, and it's this inflationary tendency that drives Sagittarius to expand his horizons to the uttermost limits.

Having set his sights, he then proceeds to explore his territory to the full. The journey may take him all his life. His territory may be physical (Sagittarius is the inveterate traveller of the Zodiac, and he may spend time living abroad from the country of his birth), or it may be territory of the mind.

It's usually the latter. Sagittarius is a seeker of wisdom. Not, it must be said, so that he can bask in a self-congratulatory glow at his own cleverness, but so that he can disseminate and promulgate that wisdom. So that he can teach. So that he can hand on the torch.

For such a happy-go-lucky, optimistic, and easy-going person, Sagittarius is surprisingly highly principled, ethical and idealistic. He has a strong sense of justice and truth. His insistence on speaking the truth can lead him into tactlessness, but there is never any deliberate intention to cause pain. He may offend through carelessness, but never callousness. He is generous, affectionate and invariably good-humoured.

In love, Sagittarius is just as casual, just as light-hearted as in every other department of his life. He's rarely romantic. Unpossessive, he prefers not to commit himself devotedly to one partner who might try to tie him down. He is a free spirit who must move through life and its myriad experiences untrammelled, answerable to no one.

Sagittarius's interests are far-ranging, and he needs constant stimulus. A Mutable Fire Sign, he can change direction easily and enthusiastically. He can plan ahead with vision and insight, for Jupiter allows him to see the 'big picture' – the overall result at which he can aim himself, straight and true, like the arrow of his glyph.

Buoyant, exuberant Jupiter encourages Sagittarius to be not only the philosopher but also the clown of the Zodiac. He has a great sense of humour and a warm, generous – even extravagant – nature. He knows how to enjoy himself, how to have fun, and likes to give pleasure to his many friends.

He's always ready for a new experience, a new adventure, and there's nothing he's afraid to tackle, and nowhere he's afraid to go. For Sagittarius, the journey is everything. For Sagittarius, it really is better to travel hopefully than to arrive.

♑ CAPRICORN

Negative · Cardinal Earth · Symbolized by The Goat

*The driving force of Cardinality, the materialism
and practicality of the Earth Element, and
the conservatism of Saturn, all combine in the
Tenth Sign: Capricorn.*

RULED BY SATURN, the Goat sees the world as a harsh and exacting arena. She expects to have to work hard to achieve what she wants, and wastes no time (or emotion) in hoping for easy options. Concealed behind her reserved exterior lies icy-cold ambition, and she uses whatever means are at her disposal in order to reach her ultimate goal: success in her chosen field.

Capricorn is astrologically obliged to exercise patience, though, for Saturn's nature is to delay and defer, and sometimes deny. But she's got time. Capricorn is frequently long-lived, remaining hale and hearty well into old age, and Saturn is inclined to give its gifts only in maturity. 'Everything comes to he who waits' is Capricorn's motto. So she works slowly and steadily onwards – and upwards, for Capricorn is determined to reach the top, however long it may take.

Status and prestige are important to Capricorn. She seeks to improve herself and to earn respect for her achievements. But she's not looking to be a 'flash in the pan' success – she needs the security of firm foundations, concrete form, long-term growth, permanence.

Much the same considerations apply in her personal life. She sees the commitment of marriage as a responsible step, not to be undertaken lightly. Her partner must be a fitting one, a true complement. She may even marry to improve her status (there is a tendency to snobbishness in Capricorn), or for dynastic reasons.

'Falling in love' is not an easy, frivolous matter for Capricorn. Saturn's cold nature inhibits her emotions, and she can be painfully shy, unable to risk declaring her feelings, unable to expose her inner needs. Often, Saturn can prevent her from acknowledging her true feelings, even to herself. The repressive nature of Capricorn's ruling Planet cannot be too greatly emphasized.

Saturn also accounts for Capricorn's extreme pessimism, a trait which, oddly enough, can manifest itself in the Tenth Sign as dry, and sometimes bitter, black comedy. It is the mirthless laughter of *I Pagliacci*; the tragedy of the buffoon. (Charlie Chaplin, who so expertly portrayed the 'little man' battered by life's unkindness, had the planet of joviality, Jupiter, in the Sign of Capricorn.)

Unlike Taurus, who likes to see her money stacked up in the bank for the pleasure of possession which it gives her, and Cancer, who likes to save hers for a 'rainy day' for the comforting security it gives her, Capricorn is a trader, and uses her money. In fact, she uses everything that comes her way in life; everything and anything that will enable her to climb her way, inch by inch, to the very top.

AQUARIUS

Positive · Fixed Air · Symbolized by The Water Bearer

*Ruled by Uranus, the Planet of unorthodoxy and
eccentricity, it comes as no surprise that the
Water Bearer, paradoxically, should be the symbol
for an Air Sign!*

THE ELEVENTH SIGN OF THE ZODIAC, is concerned with humanity on a wide scale, with brotherhood, the masses. It is the Sign of 'the people'. And because Aquarius is an Air Sign, and Air is the Element of the intellect, Aquarius is particularly concerned with the consciousness of 'the people'.

Whereas Saturn, Capricorn's ruler, has a constrained and reactionary nature, Uranus is a Planet of original and revolutionary expression. Allied to the thought processes of Air, we find in Aquarius intellectual revolution – the concept of rebellion, but not the deed.

It remains a concept because Aquarius is a detached, impartial Sign, with little emotional appreciation. Aquarius will support the 'underdog' because the underdog is being treated unfairly, not because he identifies with the underdog's suffering and feels its pain. Aquarius always maintains a strictly impersonal and clinically objective viewpoint on life.

'Freedom' is important to him – freedom of thought, particularly. Aquarius finds it difficult – even impossible – to channel his thoughts into a predetermined mould and has to blaze his own trail. His ideals and ethics may not be readily understood or appreciated, but he will uphold them with great vigour and sincerity.

Uranus is associated with electricity, and Aquarius's thought processes have an electric quality to them, often arcing from one concept to another with no apparent link or common ground. Associated, through his ruling Planet, with technological advancement, Aquarius works well in the scientific field, and electronic media in particular. Technology holds no fears for him, and his cool, logical mind finds pleasure in dissecting the workings of his many gadgets and machines.

What's he like in love? Emotionally independent, and as detached and impersonal as he is in everything else, is the answer. Aquarius likes nothing better than to be involved with a group of like-minded people, and one-to-one relationships may have to take a back seat. When he does 'settle down' (if anyone as volatile and unstable as Aquarius is capable of settling down), he's inclined to view his partner as more of a very close friend than an object of blind, unreasoning passion.

If Sagittarius is the philosopher, with his dream of truth and justice for all, then Aquarius is the person who prints and distributes the leaflets; he is the one who spreads the word, the one who broadcasts the message.

Aquarius's reputation as a social and political reformer comes partly from his idealistic and liberal mind, and partly from his ability to make mankind aware of the power of the people. Perhaps it is not altogether incongruous that one astrologically destined to show the way to the masses, should nevertheless himself march to a different tune.

♓

PISCES

Negative · Mutable Water · Symbolized by The Fishes

Too often cruelly dismissed as the 'dustbin of the Zodiac',
Pisces – the Twelfth Sign - is a rich amalgam of
everything that has gone before.

RULED BY SENSITIVE NEPTUNE, Pisces is highly impressionable and ever-changing, like her Element, Water. Whereas Saturn's function is to define boundaries, Neptune's function is to dissolve those boundaries; to liquefy the differences; to make everything *one*.

Although it is simple to say that, in Pisces, we see the urge to reach beyond the known material world to unite with the infinite, it is not so simple to understand. However, in normal everyday terms, the concept of 'universal love' manifests itself in Pisces as a deep and profound compassion, universal sympathy. Pisces hears the silent screams, and weeps for the world's suffering.

Pisces is an extremely 'giving' person, to the point of self-sacrifice, even martyrdom. She will unconsciously and instinctively put you and your needs way before her own, and nothing is too much trouble for her. She is totally unselfish. Unfortunately, however, there is the possibility that her self-effacing humility can lead to a lack of self-respect or self-worth, and she may become a 'door-mat', utterly servile and debased.

A characteristic of her ruling Planet, Neptune, is to refine and idealize, and Pisces insists on seeing the good and the best in everything and everyone.

Naturally, this is extended to those whom she loves. Pisces sees the world through very rose-coloured spectacles indeed, and places her loved one on an extremely high pedestal. There is nothing she would not do for the beloved, who finds himself the object of her boundless love – adored, pampered, indulged, cherished and all but worshipped.

But, since Neptune represents both compassion and confusion, she is easily deluded and deceived by her ruling Planet into thinking she has found her ideal, and reality comes as a dreadful disappointment. All too often the beloved turns out to have feet of clay; to be simply 'human', with all the foibles to which frail flesh is heir.

Because of Neptune's nature – its desire to heighten, refine, and idealize – Pisces has a highly developed (and totally unrealistic) sense of perfection, of fantasy. Her escapist tendencies are strong. And, although she can be (and often is) tempted to escape into the muddy oblivion of drink or drugs, her stronger instincts are to swim into the clear waters of artistic creativity. With her fluid impressionability and unlimited imagination, Pisces may be a gifted actor, writer or musician. She can recreate her dream world. With her heightened sensitivity, she may also be psychic, mediumistic or otherwise spiritually evolved.

Symbolized by the Fishes swimming in opposite directions, Pisces has the choice between progressing in a material or a spiritual direction. She can be the sinner or the saint. But, whichever she chooses, she must swim through life's ocean in ever-increasing spirals, ever outwards.

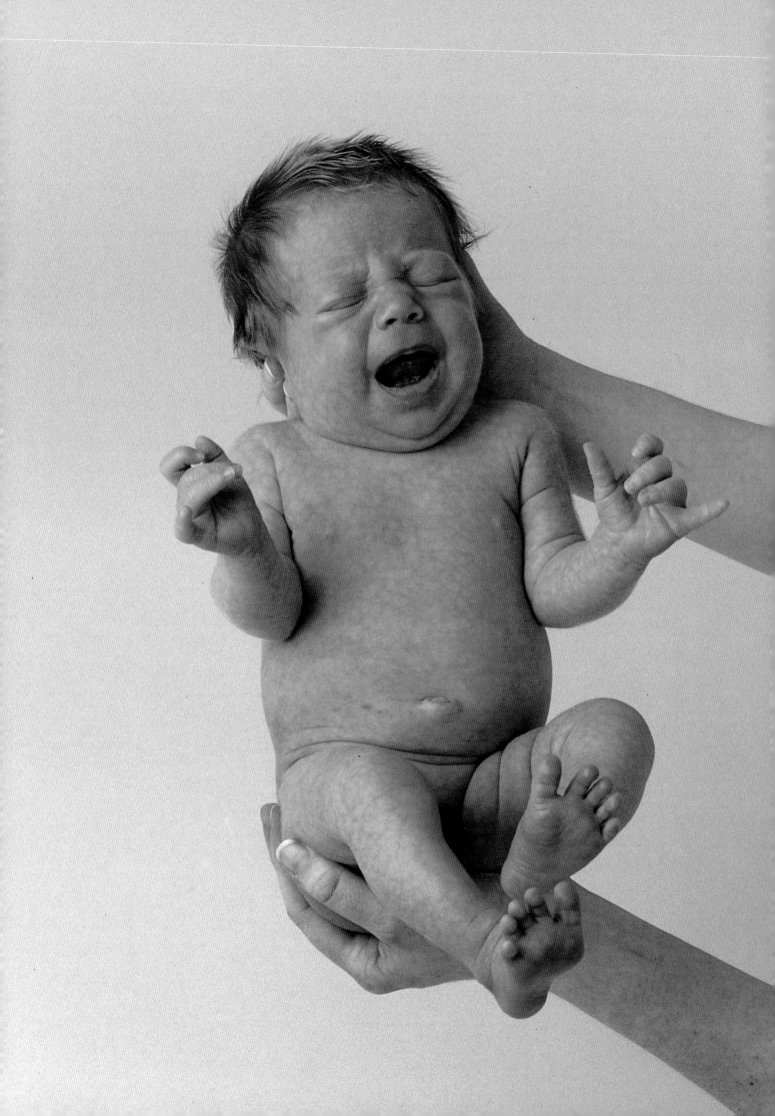

UNIQUE

unique n. Unmatched, unequalled, having no like or
equal or parallel. [(F, f. L *unicus (unus* one)]

S O FAR, WE'VE LOOKED AT YOUR SUN SIGN (which will
give an outline of some of the main characteristics of
your personality), and examined the nature of your
ruling Planet.

But there are literally tens of millions of people, worldwide, who share your Sun Sign, and it would be ludicrous
to suppose that the global population could be divided
into only twelve basic types of personality. So we must
subdivide.

Even so, there are probably still millions of people, all
over the world, who share your actual birth*day*; and probably many thousands of people who were born in the
same country as you, on the day you were born. There
may even be hundreds who were born in the same city as
you, tens born in the same town as you, on the day you
were born.

And we can subdivide even further. For – through the
medium of a horoscope – astrology allows us to examine
the nature of the moment of birth, a frozen instant of
space and time which is utterly unique.

*Your birth moment is a profound occasion. It is the
instant when you join, and irrevocably alter, the world.*
This is a simple fact, not an exaggerated claim.

Even before the umbilical cord is severed, you will
have had an irreversible effect on the Cosmos. You cannot exist in a vacuum. Because of *YOU*, two individuals
have become 'parents'. Because *YOU* have been born,
someone may live, or someone may die. Because *YOU*
have come into the world, you may in time bring forth
children who, in their turn, will make a unique and unal-
terable difference to the world. Truly, a new-born baby
bears an awesome burden of responsibility!

The likelihood of two or more babies being born at
the same instant, on the same day, in the same place –
and therefore sharing the same birth chart – is infinites-
imally small. You are unique. An individual. And because

the astrological pattern changes moment by moment,
with (like an old-fashioned kaleidoscope) an infinite number of variations, it follows that your Horoscope – the
'observation of the moment' of your birth – will be as
unique as you.

WHAT IS MEANT BY A 'PERSONAL' HOROSCOPE?

Before beginning to inspect a piece of countryside in
order to consider its suitability and potential use, a sur-
veyor has to equip himself with a map of the area. And
before you can attempt any sort of analysis of yourself –
before you can even begin to appreciate, on an objective
level, the depth and richness of your personality, your
strengths and weaknesses – you, too, will need a 'map':
your Horoscope.

It can, of course, be a map you've drawn up yourself.

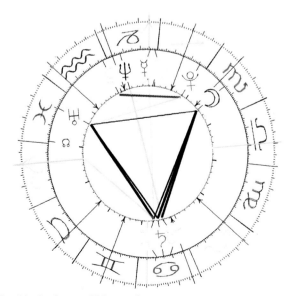

The birth chart of Nostradamus

It is a simple matter to look up your birth-date in an ephemeris (an astronomical table showing the positions of the planets), to get a rough idea of your birth chart. But remember, those positions (and that rough chart) will apply to everyone born on your birthday.

To obtain the 'Ordnance Survey' of birth maps, it is essential to have one prepared by an astrologer who can very quickly calculate (by computer) the precise planetary positions for the moment of your birth: the moment that you will share with no one else, and the pattern you will share with no one else. For the Universe is constantly moving, constantly spiralling, and the pattern is constantly changing, and will never, ever, be repeated.

A birth chart is like a 'freeze-frame' or a photograph of a planetary pattern that existed for one instant only; the pattern that is relevant solely to you. And, in order to pinpoint that pattern, we must identify the instant to which it uniquely relates: the moment of your birth.

For an accurate birth chart, knowledge of the precise time of your birth is crucial. For the time of birth will enable us to identify your Ascendant, and your Ascendant is the key which will enable us to open the door of your personality.

This, then, is your Ascendant; the key to your personality and the 'doorstep' of the First House of your Horoscope.

THE YEAR WITHIN THE DAY, AND THE ALL-IMPORTANT ASCENDANT

For the purposes of Astrology, we must forget all that we learned in science classes about astronomy. Although we know, beyond any shadow of a doubt, that the Earth moves around the Sun (taking a year for each orbit), Astrology takes the 'geocentric' viewpoint, and we must imagine that the Earth is the centre of the Solar System, and that the Sun, Moon, and Planets revolve around us.

From this artificial, geocentric viewpoint, therefore, it takes the Sun 365¼ days to 'orbit' the Earth, during which time we experience each Sign of the Zodiac from 0 degrees Aries round to 29 59 59 degrees Pisces. To this span of time, of course, we give the name 'year'.

The Earth, in actuality, is not only moving through space but also turning on its axis – one revolution every day, 365 revolutions every year. But, from our geocentric viewpoint, it appears as though the Sun revolves around us once every day.

If we imagine that the 'orbiting' Sun travels in a 'mini zodiac' surrounding the Earth, we can be exposed to all twelve Signs of the Zodiac with every daily revolution of our globe. We can experience a 'year' every twenty-four hours: a year within the day.

Because of the Earth's revolution, it is always sunrise/daybreak somewhere on the face of the globe. And every longitudinal line on the face of the globe becomes the eastern horizon (where the Sun rises) once every twenty-four hours.

For instance, dawn comes to England at the end of August round about 05.00 Greenwich Mean Time (GMT). That is the time when the Sun first appears over the eastern horizon. Dawn comes to New York roughly five hours later, at 10.00 GMT. While Londoners are enjoying a late lunch, the Earth has revolved sufficiently for the Sun to bring the beginning of a new day to Los Angeles.

Still remembering that the 'orbiting' Sun travels in the 'mini-zodiac' surrounding the Earth, dawn always breaks in the same sector of the 'mini-zodiac' as the current Sun Sign in the Zodiac proper: for instance, if you're born at daybreak on 12 August, your Sun Sign will be Leo, of course, and so will your Ascendant, or Rising Sign. The Earth revolves once every twenty-four hours. If you divide 360 (the number of degrees in a circle, or the daily rotation of the Earth and, of course, the number of degrees in the Zodiac), by the twenty-four hours in a day, you will see that the eastern horizon (the point of daybreak) sweeps over fifteen degrees every hour – one degree every four minutes. There are thirty degrees in each Sign, and so each Sign is in the Ascendant (coming up over the eastern horizon) for approximately two hours each day. The time of your birth will accurately pinpoint the precise degree of the Ascendant Sign.

It takes only four minutes for the Ascending Degree to move on from one degree to the next. In those four minutes, the whole emphasis of your Horoscope can shift and, like a celestial kaleidoscope, form a new – and totally unique – pattern.

THE HOUSES OF YOUR HOROSCOPE

First of all, what *are* the 'Houses'? And what is their particular relevance?

Earlier, we saw that your Horoscope was divided not only into twelve Signs, but also twelve Houses – a division of another layer of your Horoscope.

'Houses' are areas of life; compartments of experience; which show us *where* the energies of each Planet are expressed.

The Planets represent different energies and principles, and they are modified by the twelve different natures of the Zodiacal Signs into which they fall in your chart. And the Houses describe what departments of your life are activated by these Sign-modified Planets.

In a nutshell, if the Planets represent *what* (e.g., Venus representing your need to harmonize and relate; Mars representing your need to assert), and the Signs represent *how* (Venus in Aries harmonizes and relates in a swift and direct way; Mars in Capricorn asserts in a controlled and constructive way), then the Houses show *where* – in what area of life – the action takes place.

For instance, Saturn (the Planet that controls and consolidates) denotes the need for order and structure. But *where* is this need expressed? In which House does Saturn fall? If it's in your Third House of Mentality and Communication, you'll need facts and figures, precision of meaning, rather than 'waffle'. If it's in your Fifth House of Pleasure, you'll find that Saturn enforces rigid controls over your ability to 'let your hair down' and relax.

By looking at a birth chart we can see – from the position of the Planets in the various Signs, and the aspects (stressful or helpful) that they make to one another – if, say, someone has the potential to be a bully. But *where*

does he express those bullying traits? In his relationships (Seventh House)? Is he a tyrant at home (Fourth House)? Or is he harsh and overbearing in his career (Tenth House)?

There are many systems of House division. The most popular – certainly in the UK and the USA – is Placidus, but, over the past thirty years, the Koch system has become widely accepted, on both sides of the Atlantic.

However, there's absolutely nothing whatsoever wrong with Equal House – it's simplicity itself, and good for astrological 'beginners' to learn on. With this system (unlike others, which give Houses of unequal size), your chart will be divided into twelve equal portions; the 'cusp' (or 'door' into the next House) being the same degree as the Ascendant (the 'door' of your First House). Thus, if your Ascendant is, say, 6 degrees of Libra, then the cusp or beginning of your Second House will be 6 degrees of Scorpio. And so on.

The Houses of your Horoscope begin with the Ascendant. This is the precise degree of the Sign on the eastern horizon of the place where you were born, when you were born.

Calculating the Ascendant is a fairly tricky business, involving logarithms, tables of planetary movements, twenty minutes of your time, and possibly a couple of paracetamol! So it's far quicker, easier and far more *accurate* to let your friendly local astrologer calculate this by computer in a matter of seconds. A computer chart calculation programme can determine the planetary positions very precisely, and the process is entirely headache-free.

The complicated part is over now. With your chart in hand, your Ascendant identified, you're ready to explore the Houses of *your* Horoscope!

Division of a Horoscope by House

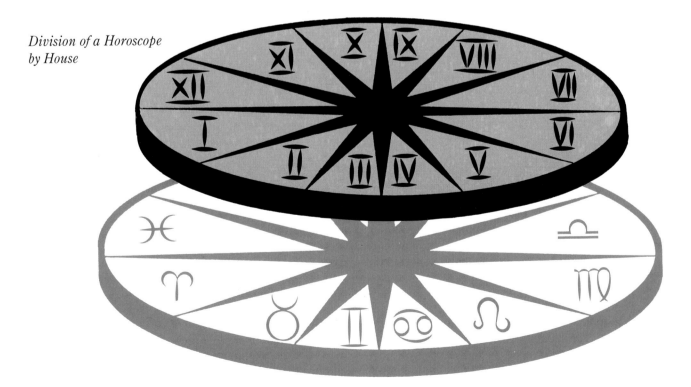

THE EASTERN HORIZON

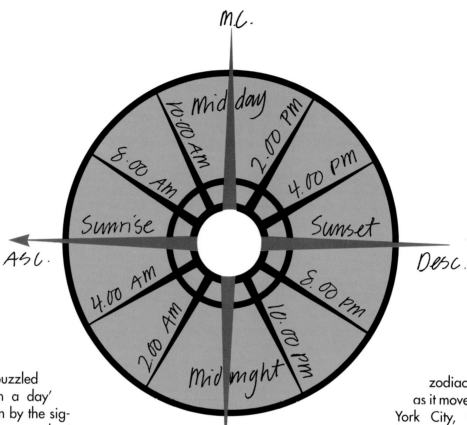

If you're still puzzled by the 'year in a day' concept, or even by the significance of the eastern horizon in your chart, try to imagine that the Earth is stationary, and that a 'mini-zodiac' revolves around the Earth. You must imagine, too, that the Sun moves round the Earth each day.

Dawn – daybreak – occurs in the same Sign of the 'mini-zodiac' as the actual Zodiac. Wherever you find the Sun, you find the Sign of the month, and the Sign of the moment. The Sun 'travels round the Earth' in that Sign. So, if you were born at daybreak – the point when the Sun first appears on the eastern horizon – during, say, the month-long Sign of Sagittarius, your Ascendant will fall in the Sign of Sagittarius, too.

The Sun climbs into the sky on its journey 'round the world', taking the dawn to the west. Wherever the Sun is, will be dawn and the eastern horizon *somewhere* on the globe. The Sun's position, of course, is totally relative to one's viewpoint. To a Londoner, the overhead Sun spells midday, but at the same time it's midnight to an Australian.

So a baby born (for example, in London) at dawn on any day during the month of, say, Aries, will have an Aries Ascendant. The Sun takes Aries in the 'mini-zodiac' along with it as it moves towards New York City, USA. Another baby may be born in London at noon on the same day. The Sun (still in the Sign of Aries) has moved west, towing the 'mini-zodiac' after it, and leaving Cancer on the eastern horizon of the babies' birthplace. That second baby, therefore, will have a Cancer Ascendant. A third baby is born at sunset, by which time the Sun will be moving over the Pacific, bringing dawn towards New Zealand and the Fiji Islands, and pulling the 'mini-zodiac' even further round. Our sunset baby will have Libra Rising. An Aries baby born at midnight will have a Capricorn Ascendant.

Confirm these rough computations with your computer chart. Born at daybreak? The Sun will be near/in the same Sign as the Ascendant, the eastern horizon of your chart. Born at midday? The Sun will be in the Tenth House, the southern part of your chart. Sunset? You'll find the Sun around your Seventh House, the cusp of which is called the 'Descendant'. A midnight baby? Look for the Sun in your Fourth House, the northern part of your chart.

Incidentally, in case you were wondering, in Astrology the eastern horizon is on the left of your chart!

SUN SIGN DATES AND THE SIGNIFICANCE OF THE CUSPS

Let's conclude Part One by clearing up a potential source of confusion – the cusps. It's entirely possible of course that you may be trying to interpret your chart without really being sure what your SUN sign is. The moment when the Sun enters each of the twelve divisions (Signs) of the Zodiac each year is astronomically determined, and this information is readily available from an ephemeris, or planetary timetable.

Generally speaking, though, the dates for the Sun's occupation of each of the Signs is roughly as follows:

ARIES	21st March to 20th April
TAURUS	21st April to 21st May
GEMINI	22nd May to 21st June
CANCER	22nd June to 23rd July
LEO	24th July to 23rd August
VIRGO	24th August to 23rd September
LIBRA	24th Sepember to 23rd October
SCORPIO	24th October to 22nd November
SAGITTARIUS	23rd November to 21st December
CAPRICORN	22nd December to 20th January
AQUARIUS	21st January to 19th February
PISCES	20th February to 20th March

If you are born on or near to the dates given above you may feel doubtful about your true Sun Sign. You may wonder why you fit the description of, say, Cancer, when the newspaper 'star sign' columns have delineated you a Leo. It is popularly known as being born 'on the cusp'.

Contrary to popular opinion, being born on the cusp does not mean you are a mixture of both Signs.

In the course of a year (one circuit of the Zodiac) the Sun travels 360 degrees, but it's easier to say '19 degrees of Gemini' rather than '79 degrees', so the Zodiac is divided into twelve units of 30 degrees each. When the Sun has travelled through 30 degrees of Aries, it enters Taurus. When it has travelled through the 30 degrees of Taurus, it enters Gemini. The cusp itself is nothing but a dividing point between Signs, and has no character of its own.

A light cannot be half on and, at the same time, half off. It must be one or ther other. If your Sun is positioned at 29 degrees, 59 minutes and 59 seconds of Sagittarius, you're a Sagittarius. One second later, though, and the Sun will be at 0 degrees of Capricorn, and you'll be a Goat, not an Archer.

The problem of 'cuspal confusion' is caused by the fact that the Sun enters each Sign at slightly different times, and often different days of the month, every year.

Obviously it's important to find out your Sun Sign if you're born on the cusp, otherwise you might spend a lifetime wondering why you don't display the characteristics of, for instance, the freedom-loving and freaky Aquarius you always thought you were supposed to be, when all along you've been a dreamy idealistic Pisces. Or, say, why you're a deep and secretive Scorpio, when all the newspaper 'star sign' columns suggest you're an open and happy-go-lucky Sagittarius.

But if in doubt, check it out. Your local astrologer can quickly and easily determine your true Sun Sign if you're born around any of the dates listed in the chart on the left. You have no reason or excuse for sitting on the fence – or the cusp!

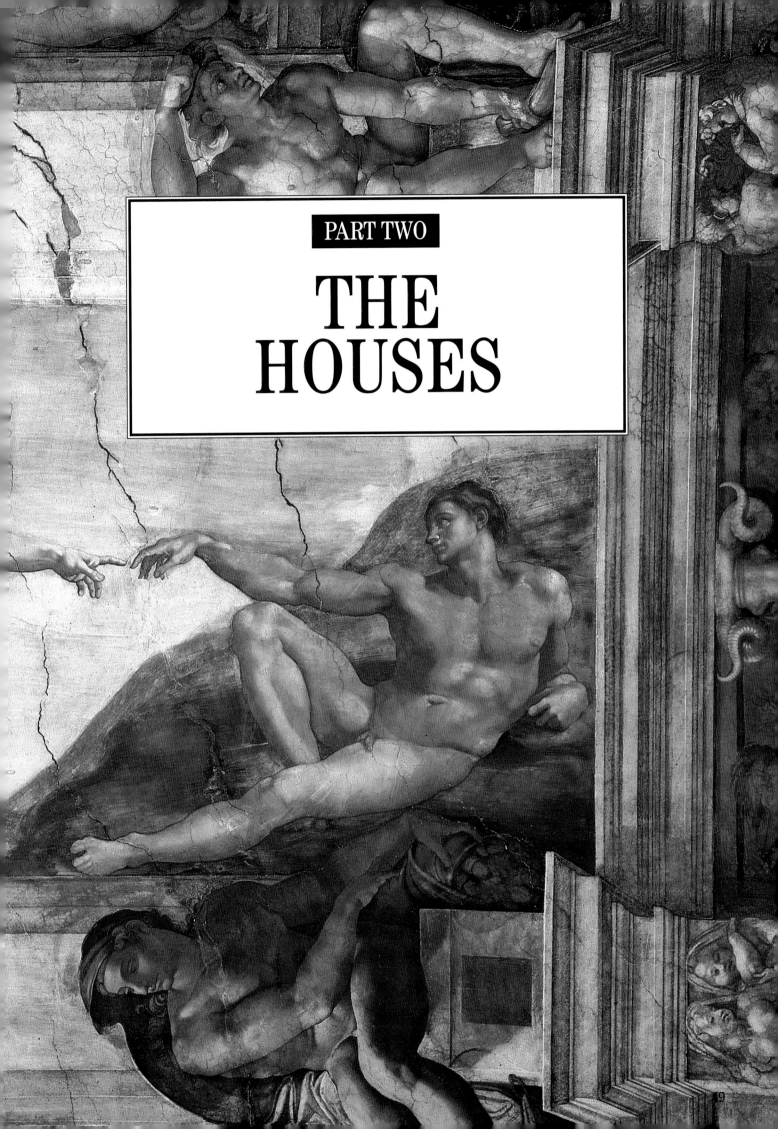

PART TWO

THE HOUSES

THE ASCENDANT –
CUSP OF THE FIRST HOUSE

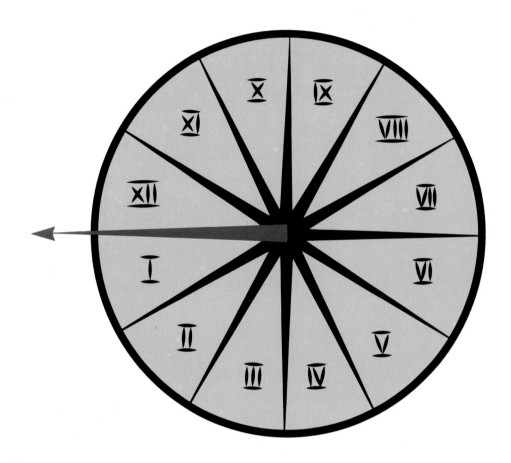

EVER WONDERED WHY people don't match the textbook descriptions of their Sun Sign characteristics? Ever been puzzled as to why your Leo friend, who should be ebullient and outgoing, is so serious and cautious? Or why your Cancer neighbour, who ought to be home-loving and maternal, is so restless? Why your supposedly decisive, go-ahead Aries child takes such a long time to come to a decision? You haven't been reading the wrong books. You've simply met the Ascendant, or Rising Sign.

As you know, every twenty-four hours each of the Signs of the Zodiac moves over any given point on the globe, and your Ascendant is the precise degree of the Sign which was moving over the eastern horizon of your birth-place at the precise moment you were born. To calculate it, all you need to know is your date, place and time of birth. The more accurate your birth-time, the more precise and detailed your birth chart, or Horoscope, will be.

Your Ascendant is one of the factors that makes you different from the millions of people, worldwide, who share your birthday. It marks the beginning of the individual Horoscope and is the 'doorstep' or threshold of the First House.

It has been said that if your Sun Sign is the message that you have to give to the world, then your Ascendant is the *style* in which you deliver that message.

The Ascendant is the set of characteristics that you present to the outside world, and to which other people relate to initially, before they get to know your Sun Sign – your core personality.

It is an astrological 'overcoat'. Your cautious Leo friend may wear the cashmere or Harris tweed of a Capricorn Ascendant; your restless Cancer neighbour may have the travel-stained and out-at-elbow mackintosh of Sagittarius Rising slung round her shoulders; and your Aries child may have agonized for hours over which of his Libra jackets to put on. The Ascendant is what other people see first.

Not only can the Ascendant show the outer manner of a person, it also gives an indication of certain physical characteristics.

♈ To **Aries Rising** it often gives the famed red hair which we have come to associate with Mars. If your Ascendant is in the Sign of Aries, you are likely to be of medium height, and to have a sturdy frame and a muscular body. You may display amazing surges of strength when the need arises – you're great to have around when there's an unco-operative pickle jar to open!

Aries rules the head, and your forehead may be broad, with eyebrows shaped like the glyph for Aries – they may even meet over the bridge of your nose. Your eyes have a very 'direct' look – you may have been told off for 'staring' when you were a child. You maintain eye-contact when talking to people.

If you have an Aries Ascendant, then the ruler of your chart (*not* the same as the ruler of your Sun Sign) is the Planet Mars. A principle of Mars is to quicken every-thing it touches, and so you are likely always to be in a hurry, and this may show itself in your gait. Your head will jut forward (you may even walk at a slight forward-projecting angle), as though it's anxious to get where you're going long before your body.

Because Aries rules the head, and Mars is the Planet associated with anger and violence, you may be acci-dent-prone, sustaining injuries to your face and head. Facial cuts and bruises are the hallmark of Aries Rising!

Mars will also quicken your mental responses. If your hasty Mars temper does not have an opportunity to express itself, it may turn inwards, leading to fulminat-ing headaches, migraine, brainstorms. Sport or hard physical exercise is an excellent release – far better to sweat out your Mars!

You share an Aries Ascendant with Bette Midler, John Lennon, and Barbra Streisand.

An Aries Ascendant accounts for Barbra Streisand's initial image as pushy and aggressive. The strong determination of her Taurus Sun, allied to the Martian qualities of force and impetus, aided her in her battle for financial backing for her film, Yentl

Bette Midler – who seems to glory in her loud, brash, and totally unsubtle Aries Rising image!

♉ **Taurus Rising** lends a mildly bovine quality to the bone structure and physical characteristics. Born with your Ascendant in the Sign of Taurus, you will have a well-shaped body, which may have a tendency to thicken or gain weight as you get older. (Taurus and calories seem very attracted to each other.) Your shoulders will be strong and solid, and your head oblong in shape.

If Venus has been kind to you, the ox-like build which is sometimes associated with this Rising Sign will be less apparent.

A Taurus Ascendant often bestows an air of lush ripeness, a warm, rich attractiveness that owes little to conventional beauty.

Your skin will be clear and smooth, and you'll have a placid expression, and a lazy, gentle smile. Lady Bulls can be skilled in the application of cosmetics, and many male Bulls sport carefully tended designer stubble! But your outstanding facial feature is most likely to be your eyes – big and beautiful, and with no need for false eyelashes!

Because Taurus rules the throat area, you may have a pleasant and melodious voice which is pitched fairly low for ordinary speech. In anger, though, this can easily change to a bellow!

Venus will give you a liking for pastels and soft colours, and you'll have good dress sense. Your home will be comfortable, and extremely tastefully decorated and furnished, courtesy of your chart ruler.

You share a Taurus Ascendant with the splendid comedienne and actress, Mae West.

Ⅱ The most youthful-looking member of the Zodiac is **Gemini Rising**.

If you have a Gemini Ascendant, then spritely Mercury is your chart ruler and the Planet responsible for your 'Peter Pan' image.

Mercury won't let you sit still for a minute. It produces an abundance of nervous energy, and you are consequently 'highly strung'. Always active, you don't have a chance to relax and put on weight: you burn off almost every calorie that passes your lips, and so fat has little opportunity to settle on your wiry frame.

Facially, your features are neat and somewhat sharp. However, many people born when Gemini moved over the eastern horizon of their birth place display a strongly idiosyncratic profile, where the forehead and chin slope away from the nose and mouth, rather like a cricket.

The eyes of Gemini Rising are always on the move. When you talk to someone, your eyes are continually darting round the room. You are extremely observant, and you miss very little of what is going on, able to assimilate information from two or more simultaneous conversations.

Not only are your eyes busy, your hands are, too, for you gesticulate as you talk – and you talk very rapidly! You seem to have more to say (and say it more quickly) than any other Sign. You're also an excellent mimic, and may have a flair for languages.

In dress you like bright colours, and enjoy mixing patterns and fabrics. You love lapel pins and badges, and enjoy wearing bizarre jewellery – the more the merrier !

Like you, Rolling Stone Mick Jagger has a Gemini Ascendant.

Taurus rules the neck, and male Bulls generally take an extraordinarily large collar size! If you have Taurus Rising in your birth chart, the likelihood is that your neck is thick and short, unless Venus (your chart ruler) has taken pity on you! In which case, you'll have a long, slender, almost swan-like neck, on which you'll hold your head well. Your carriage is likely to be graceful, and your feet and hands will be small and neat.

The glyph for the Sign of Cancer is also a pictograph for the breasts, and **Cancer Rising** gives an emphasis to this area of the body. Cancer Rising females are generally big-breasted, while males tend to be 'top-heavy' with a broad, fleshy chest, and relatively narrow hips.

You are unlikely to be above medium height and, unfortunately, there is a strong tendency to gain weight later in life. You are not the most energetic of creatures, and are rarely found 'working-out' at the local gymnasium, or playing sport. Of course, your disinterest in participating in sport may spring from the fact that your frame is not built for speed – although your shoulders would ensure you'd make a good Rugby or American football player! Any interest in sport is likely to be confined to watching it on TV.

Your face is likely to be round, with a pale complex-ion. The skin may be sensitive, or delicate. Your cheeks will be chubby, your mouth soft and well-shaped, and your eyes will be round and 'innocent'-looking. But the best description of Cancer Rising will be found by consulting your chart ruler – the Moon! The 'Man in the Moon' (whose face can be clearly observed once a month, at Full Moon) has a soft and tender appearance, with eyes full of concern and quiet reflection.

When you move, you tend to scuttle quickly from place to place, in a series of zigzags. You never approach your objective in a direct line.

You're not the most fashionable of dressers, preferring the comfort (and security) of tried-and-tested clothes that have been in your wardrobe for years.

Big-breasted film star Jayne Mansfield, and former 'Mr Universe' Arnie Schwarzenegger share your Cancer Ascendant.

Jayne Mansfield, with the soft and well-shaped mouth, tender appearance (and the well-developed chest) which is typical of Cancer Rising

Marilyn Monroe's Leo Ascendant lends glamour and 'star' quality to her Gemini Sun

There's no mistaking **Leo Rising**, from the minute the Lion walks through the door.
A Leo Ascendant imparts an almost 'regal' quality, and this is most noticeable in posture and carriage. Your back will be ramrod-straight, your head held proudly, and your walk will be slow, deliberate and 'majestic'. When you enter a room, you will invariably pause for a second on the threshold – framed in the doorway – in order that people will notice you. You don't simply 'go into' a room: you most definitely 'make an entrance'!

You are likely to be taller than average, and well-built. Irrespective of whether or not you are fashion-conscious, you have an eye for design and a sense of glamour, and may wear bright pronounced patterns and strong colours.

Your crowning glory is your hair – 'mane' is an apt description – and you are very vain about it. Male Lions were in the vanguard of the ponytail fashion, while Lionesses generally have huge amounts of very long hair, carefully styled to look thick and abundant. You are constantly fiddling with your hair, shaking or sweeping it back, and running your fingers through it and generally drawing attention to it.

Facially, you are likely to be strong featured, and you radiate a sunny glow of inner confidence.

Born with Leo Rising, the Sun is your chart ruler. And (irrespective of your actual birthdate-defined Sun Sign) if you were born when the Sun powered its way over the horizon, you'll be charged with the strength and power of the most important body in the Solar System – the celestial 'battery'. Leo Rising has great presence, and no one – but no one – outshines you!

You share a Leo Ascendant with that epitome of radiant glamour, the film star Marilyn Monroe.

♍ Although **Virgo Rising** shares the same chart ruler (Mercury) as Gemini, the physical characteristics are not the same. For Gemini is an Air Sign, making the Mercurial influence light and cerebral, whereas in Virgo the Planet is 'grounded' by Virgo's Element, Earth.

Virgo Rising usually presents a calm, ordered and neat appearance.

You are likely to be meticulous in your dress, and always well-groomed and band-box smart. You were, seemingly, born with a clothes-brush in your hand! You like cool, sober colours (navy blue is a particular favourite) and you prefer practical and serviceable clothes in uncomplicated, unfussy styles, and your accessories always correctly complement your outfit.

Your features are well-defined and generally pleasing, and your face has an animated expression. You may not be overwhelmingly pretty, but your looks will be classic, with a fine bone structure. The overall impression you give is one of elegance. Your voice may be rather clipped and precise.

Not for you the lavish locks of Leo! Virgo Rising prefers a well-cut hairstyle – a simple bob or a 'short-back-and-sides' – with, of course, a very precise parting! Your hair is always scrupulously clean and well-conditioned.

You have good posture, and physical stamina, but you do not have a very easy stride. You walk 'from the knees' in a rather stilted manner, and consequently you take many more steps than, say, long-legged Sagittarius who swings his legs from the hip. Your feet are small, neat and shapely.

The elegant Marlene Dietrich shares a Virgo Ascendant with you.

The cool, classic Virgo Rising looks of Capricorn Marlene Dietrich

From the classic looks of a Virgo Ascendant, we turn to the sheer *prettiness* of **Libra Rising**. With Venus as your chart ruler, you will be extremely attractive, with looks that the opposite sex may find quite irresistible! And that's not all, for Venus generally ensures that Libra Rising allies good looks with a warm personality and a charming nature. In fact, you should thank your lucky stars that Libra was rising over the eastern horizon when you were born!

You are likely to be of medium height, or a little below (all good things come in small parcels, they say) and to have a shapely, well-proportioned body. You move very gracefully, seeming to glide from place to place, with an easy carriage.

Your skin is likely to be fair, with a translucent sheen, and you've probably been lucky enough to avoid the pitfalls of skin blemishes like acne. Instead of pockmarks, Venus gives you dimples!

Bones will be delicate, features refined and symmetrical. Physically, everything about you is pleasing to the eye. And, talking of eyes, yours are likely to be extremely attractive – large, clear, wide-set, and a beautiful colour. You have a warm and gentle smile, well-shaped lips and a generous mouth.

All this physical bounty from Venus does have a drawback, though. It's called vanity. You're extremely aware of your own attractiveness, and have a tendency to use beauty as the yardstick by which to judge others – forgetting that beauty is only skin deep.

You share your Libra Ascendant (and dimples!) with Dolly Parton, David Bowie, Elizabeth Taylor, Nancy Reagan and Rod Stewart.

Above: Nancy Reagan: well-shaped lips and a generous mouth

Left: Delicate bones, refined features, and fair skin. David Bowie – The Thin White Duke

♏ After the 'chocolate box' prettiness of the Libra Ascendant come the dark and brooding looks of **Scorpio Rising**.

With Pluto as your chart ruler, the overwhelming impression you give is of quietly contained power. Your figure has been drawn with economy of line, and your lithe body is well structured. You walk silently, and all your movements are made in a controlled way.

You belong to the Henry Ford School of Fashion: everything you wear is black. Clothes are prized for their dramatic value; anything that enhances the mystique that surrounds you, like long swirling cloaks, veiled hats, satin elbow-length gloves (black, naturally) will be a wardrobe favourite. You practically invented the concept of power dressing, although you don't have to resort to it – it would simply be icing on the cake.

Your hair will be coarse and abundant. Its colour is likely to be very dark – even black – and you'll have strongly marked eyebrows. It is also likely that you'll have a large (but not fleshy), well-sculpted nose, and a strong jaw-line. Your most outstanding facial feature, though, will be your eyes.

In the Zodiac, the eyes of Scorpio Rising are unequalled. Whatever their colour – dark brown or bright blue – they have a piercing, penetrating quality, like laser beams. You may have noticed that many people are unable to meet the directness of your gaze, almost as if they were afraid that if they did, you would be able to discern what they were thinking. Scorpio Rising has the power to instil fear and apprehension.

Hypnotic eyes, a magnetic voice, a commanding personality, veiled (but potent) sexuality and an air of mystery – that's Scorpio Rising!

You share a Scorpio Ascendant with the performer, Prince, and the power shoulder pads of Bette Davis, Joan Crawford and Margaret Thatcher.

Opposite: The diminutive, dimpled and delightful Dolly Parton
Above left: The powerful, brooding Plutonian looks of actress Joan Crawford.
Above: Prince – always seen in immensely dramatic clothes

If Virgo Rising is the astrological 'neatpot', then **Sagittarius Rising** has to be the 'Shambler' of the Zodiac.

'Casual' is the best word for your wardrobe. You probably live in jeans and sweatshirts, and feel very uncomfortable at the prospect of having to dress up in formal clothes. However, when you do make the effort, you can look absolutely stunning. There are one or two really bizarre outfits lurking in your wardrobe, which you'll wear occasionally.

Sagittarius, the Archer, is represented as a Centaur (half man, half horse), and Sagittarius Rising is very coltish in behaviour and appearance.

Your chart ruler, Jupiter, has influence over the hips and thighs, and so you will have disproportionately long legs. This doesn't necessarily mean you will be excessively tall, but you will probably be well over medium height.) Your limbs generally will be 'gangling' and awkward, and at times, you seem unsure what to do with them. There is a tendency to clumsiness in childhood.

Restless, you pace up and down when you're thinking, and you have a very jaunty walk, bouncing on the balls of your feet, and springing up and down like a yo-yo.

Your build is likely to be slim in youth, but Jupiter's expansionary nature could put up a battle in middle age. Your face will be long and open, and you are likely to have the characteristic Sagittarian lantern jaw. You probably have good, even teeth, and nice eyes with many laughter lines crinkled round them.

But by far and away your best feature is your wide and dazzling smile, which can illuminate the whole of your face.

You share a Sagittarius Ascendant (and a radiant smile) with Diana, Princess of Wales, Goldie Hawn, Elvis Presley, and Jimi Hendrix.

Left: Unlike the Centaur (half man, half horse), the symbol of her Rising Sun, the adorable Goldie Hawn has the body of a woman and face of a innocent child. But it's the dazzling smile of her Sagittarius Ascendant that lights up her entire face.

Opposite: A force to be reckoned with. Bette Davis – Aries Sun, with Scorpio Rising.

To have **Capricorn Rising** means that the planetary ruler of your chart is Saturn, and Saturn rules the bones.

With a Capricorn Ascendant, you're likely to be big- or heavily-boned, with a short, stocky build. The 'heavy' influence of Saturn may mean poor posture and rounded shoulders. There may be a tendency to arthritic complaints. The emphasis on bones means good teeth, and yours will probably be very strong and white. Your complexion may be fairly dark.

Saturn is the Planet of old age, and life for you gets better after forty. You 'lighten up', both in looks and personality, and may become positively frivolous!

As a baby, you were wrinkled and ugly, and probably looked like Sir Winston Churchill. As a child, you were serious and old for your years; and as a young adult you probably looked gloomy. But the older you get, the better-looking you become. You manage to look younger with every passing year, without the assistance of expensive creams and lotions!

You dress conservatively, in classic styles and sober colours, and prefer natural materials, shunning synthetics. Rich Goats always wear designer-label clothes and handmade shoes. You may not be in the 'designer' league but you would prefer one *haute couture* dress, or bespoke suit (even from a thrift shop) to half a dozen ready-made, 'off-the-peg' garments. Your favourite colour is grey.

You share your Capricorn Ascendant with Paul Getty and Buddy Holly.

Capricorn Rising has a preference for classic styles. Conservatism in cut and colour is the hallmark of a Capricorn Ascendant. Right: Paul Getty.

Opposite: Buddy Holly – Capricorn Rising's idea of outrageous dressing!

Aquarius Rising can sometimes present a rather bizarre appearance – aptly, for a Sign ruled by the unorthodox Planet Uranus!

You are probably taller than most people, with a slim, spare frame and slender limbs. Your head may be somewhat larger than average, and you'll have good bone structure, with interesting planes to your face. Your complexion is probably pale.

Your dress sense can best be described as eclectic, and may earn you a reputation for eccentricity. You like bright, electric colours and never play safe with quiet shades. Nor do you dress your age. (In fact, you could lay money that the pensioner you see at the Darby and Joan Club, dressed in baseball boots, Levis and cerise sweater has Aquarius Rising!) Or you may prefer army fatigues, leather and chains, or an exclusive wardrobe of good old denim.

With an Aquarius Ascendant, your hair will be a distinguishing feature. You're never afraid to experiment at the beauty salon or the barber's, and your hair is likely to be eye-catching (even traffic-stopping!) – big and bushy, whether permed and curly, short and spiky, long and shaggy, dyed all colours of the rainbow, or prematurely grey! Not content with this, male Water Bearers often sport beards or massive side-burns.

An Aquarius Ascendant also means extraordinary eyes. If you were born under Uranus's influence, your eyes will slope sharply downwards (rather like a bloodhound's). Your eyebrows will be either finely arched, or will resemble two caterpillars crawling over your face. You have strong, arresting features.

You share your Aquarius Ascendant with singer Jim Morrison, and revolutionary Fidel Castro.

Above: The strong, arresting features of Jim Morrison

Many male Water Bearers sport beards.
Opposite: Fidel Castro

⊬ With **Pisces Rising**, the emphasis is once again on the eyes.

If you were born when Pisces was shimmering over the eastern horizon of your birth-place, then watery Neptune is your chart ruler. Neptune holds dominion over the sea and everything that moves in it – and that includes fish!

Fish-like eyes are a dominant physical characteristic in a Pisces Ascendant. Yours will be big and lustrous, and either very pale or very dark. Whereas the eyes of Gemini twinkle, yours will glisten and shine and have a moist appearance. These are the 'twin pools' of love poems!

Apart from your eyes, your face in general is likely to be extremely attractive, with a sweet smile and full, rather protuberant lips. A Pisces Ascendant tends to give a translucent quality to the complexion: fair-skinned Fishes are very pale; dark-skinned Fishes have a ripe, lush skin tone.

Your chart ruler gives you the ability to merge with your surroundings and blend into the background, and so you choose clothes that won't call attention to yourself. You like to wear greens and blues, and prefer clothes that are soft, comfortable and easy to wear, rather than fashionable and gimmicky (filmy, floaty materials are especial favourites).

You probably spend hours in front of the mirror trying to cope with your hair. There may be plenty of it, but it's likely to be very fine and therefore difficult to manage.

You are of medium height and build, with a typically Neptunian way of moving: you simply shimmer into view, with a silent and effortless gliding movement, almost as though you were on castors – but it's more likely to have something to do with your excessively large feet!

You share your Pisces Ascendant (and your beautiful eyes) with Princess Caroline of Monaco, Gregory Peck, Sophia Loren, Henry Fonda, Raquel Welch, Robert Redford and Whitney Houston.

Aries Gregory Peck (top), Taurus Henry Fonda (below), and Aquarius Princess Caroline of Monaco (opposite) all have an Ascendant in the Sign of Pisces. All three have exceptionally beautiful eyes – one of the benefits of Pisces Rising

THE
FIRST HOUSE

So far, we have looked at only the cusp of the First House – a point more commonly called the 'Ascendant'.

The importance of the Ascendant cannot be overemphasized, nor in any way denied. It is the most sensitive part of your Horoscope, colouring your whole personality. The Sign in which your Ascendant falls can be considered even more crucial in the process of understanding yourself than your Sun Sign (the Sign delineated by your birthday) – the sign which, until now, may have been your only insight into the richness of your individuality.

The First House of Personality and Self is totally and solely concerned with you, personally.

As we have seen, the Ascendant describes the style of your personality, your physical attributes, mannerisms and idiosyncrasies – your basic nature – as well as the kind of outlook you have. It describes the manner in which you approach your goals in life – the type of path you'll take towards your ultimate destiny (as described by your Sun Sign).

Any Planet found on or near (within eight degrees either side of) the Ascendant will play a strongly significant role in defining your character, for it contributes its planetary characteristics to the modality of the Ascending Sign.

The Ascendant, or Rising Sign, has been described as a dual lens, through which other people see you, and through which you focus your true character to the outside world.

In the First House, it's a case of 'Me, me, me' all the way. Planets located in the First House of Self and Personality play a crucial role indicating the way in which a character will unfold

It can also be thought of as a filter, through which you assimilate your experience of life. For instance, a Capricorn Ascendant may take a rather pessimistic view, but a Sagittarius Ascendant will invariably look on the bright side. A Taurus Ascendant may take pleasure from the possession of money for its own sake, while a Leo Ascendant can enjoy only what that money can buy. Some people see the doughnut; others see only the hole.

But to assume that the Ascendant says all there is to say about the First House is analogous to an estate agent who expects to negotiate the sale of a house on the strength of his description of the front door.

We are going to open that door, and cross the threshold (the Ascendant) of *your* First House.

As well as physical characteristics, the First House also describes your early years, the sort of childhood experiences you will have had; it can even give an indication of the birth moment, although corroborative significators will be necessary. But, in general terms, the presence of, say, Saturn close to the Ascendant could indicate a long and arduous birth, whereas Mars close to the Ascendant could indicate a swift one – or even a Caesarian section if other factors are present.

The Ascendant marks the moment when you joined the world, and the nature of any Planet in the First House describes the impact you made.

As we have seen, the Sun is your personal powerhouse, a kind of astrological battery or dynamo. In the First House, or conjunct (within eight degrees of) the Ascendant, the Sun's effect is especially strong. Because both your Ascendant and your Sun are in the same Sign, the nature of that Sign is doubly potent. This will increase your sense of self-awareness, and strengthen your will-power.

It's the 'larger than life' placement, for Sun in the

First energizes you to a greater degree than it does most other people – there's no way you'll be content with a seat at the back of the stadium. Of course, this massive input of astrological clout can make you overbearing, even domineering, but its positive attributes far out-weigh the negative.

In the natural Zodiac (which begins with 0 degrees Aries) the First House is naturally assigned to Aries. And so the First House of your chart – irrespective of the actual Sign on the cusp – will also carry with it a faint trace of the openness, vitality and aggression of Aries.

This additional astrological factor is beautifully illustrated by the late Bruce Lee, the martial arts expert, and Arnold Schwarzenegger, both of whom have Sun in the First. So has Paul Newman, whose charisma overrides the character of any role he plays. He may be an excellent actor but, above all else, he's a star.

A First House Sun can also be described by a computer term: WYSIWYG – What You See Is What You Get. Open, direct, you attack life with vigour and enthusiasm, and you're a natural leader. You're here to make your mark in life, and your personality will shine through, regardless.

The singer Madonna (Leo Sun) has not only the extremely apt Rising Sign of Virgo, but also the Moon exactly on the Ascendant.

The Moon in a chart represents our needs, our emotions and feelings, nurturing abilities, how we receive impressions, and also our relationship with the general public. Madonna, a shrewd businesswoman, knows exactly what the public wants from her. She revels in her role of virgin/whore for, after all, it enables her to obtain what *she* wants: self-validation through the approbation of others. This vitally necessary approval and attention

Arnold Schwarzenegger's First House Sun carries a faint trace of Martian aggression (Mars rules this House in the Natural Zodiac)

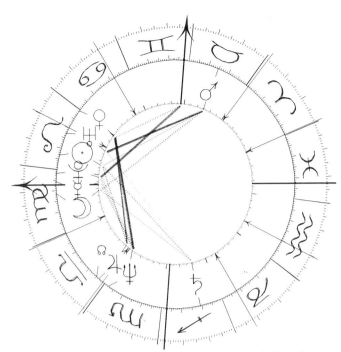

Madonna needs the acclaim of the public to reinforce her sense of self-validation

You're one of life's communicators, and it's no mere coincidence that Alexander Graham Bell, the inventor of the telephone, had Mercury in the First. So has Johnny Carson, America's best-known chat show host!

Venus in the First House, or close to the Ascendant, not only indicates a heightened sense of self-worth (for Venus represents what we find of value), but also has a delightful softening effect, conferring grace and a pleasant disposition.

This may be why the former Prime Minister Margaret Thatcher, whose Sun is in the drivingly Cardinal Sign of Libra, and whose Ascendant is in the forceful Sign of Scorpio, nevertheless enjoys a tremendous measure of personal popularity amongst her peers. (Her political policies may have been resented in many quarters, but she earned at the least grudging admiration for what she stood for.)

The controlling effect of Pluto, her chart ruler, has 'stiffened' her Venus, and Saturn on the Ascendant probably accounts for her image as 'The Iron Lady'. But when everything is said and done, Margaret Thatcher is very much a 'lady', and one who displays abundant charm in her personal relationships. She is held in great esteem throughout the world, not simply as a politician but as a woman (albeit an aggressive one!), and as one who has been a role model for her sex. The Arien flavour of the First House also means that Margaret Thatcher is a pioneer, a politician who was never afraid to lead the way.

Your First House Venus probably accounts for your generally happy memories of childhood. You were an outgoing child, with a sunny disposition, and an engaging manner. You were probably extremely attractive, and able to charm the birds from the trees!

is obtained by nurturing her fans with the food of their fantasies, thereby meeting *their* needs in return.

A First House Moon can indicate a childlike need for security and reassurance. Your early years meant a lot to you, and you will have retained vivid impressions of your childhood and family influence. You may be very close to your mother, or have a strong need for a family yourself. You are ultra-sensitive: not only in your feelings, but in your acute awareness of the feelings of others, picking up, and responding to psychic vibrations.

A First House Mercury sharpens your intellect; you are very observant, and every experience in life is grist to your mill. Whatever your ultimate destination, your path towards it is likely to lead through the field of communication, for Mercury has equipped you with the ability and drive to express yourself.

In mythology, Mars was the god of war and military strife, and Winston Churchill, who as Prime Minister led Great Britain through the Second World War, had a First House Mars.

So had HRH the Duke of Windsor (Edward VIII), whose selfish and self-centred First House Mars in Aries fired him to abandon his position as King, thus rocking the stability of the monarchy, in order to obtain what he wanted: marriage to twice-divorced Wallis Simpson.

Mars is very much at home here, for – in the Natural Zodiac – Mars-ruled Aries is on the cusp of the First House. So you're likely to have a double dose of Martian aggression, drive and initiative, regardless of the actual Sign in which your First House is placed.

Conflict is no stranger to you. From early childhood you have had to fight for what you want, and you have never willingly settled for second place.

In fact Mars is excessively aggressive, and never more so than in the First House. It is a Planet associated with competition. Many astrologers link this with sport, but Mars is not particularly sporting. Indeed it has little concept of fair play. It holds no truck with the idea that the important thing is not whether you win or lose, but how you play the game. To Mars, winning is everything. There is no glory in coming second, and Mars takes little pleasure in wearing the silver medal.

A First House Mars motivates you to win through, whatever the odds, whatever the cost. To come first, to be Number One is everything. Others may have their fifteen minutes of fame under the spotlight, but you have to be permanently at the front of Life's stage. Fuelled by the energy of Mars, there is little doubt that you'll get there.

Jupiter in the First House means you come into the world sublimely confident. Imbued with Jupiter's optimism, faith and enthusiasm, you are convinced of your ability to enthuse and excite others, but you must guard against your tendency to promise more than you may be able to deliver. You have unparalleled vision, and always have your sights set on the 'big picture'. Others may suffer from poverty of aspiration, but not First House Jupiter.

Jupiter confers dignity and wisdom, and you will be seen as a wise and benevolent leader. You may even have a role to play as some sort of moral, spiritual or philosophical authority.

Jupiter inflates all it touches, and so you may have a commanding physical stature, or a larger than life personality. Maria Callas, the opera singer, is a good example. Both her Sun and Jupiter conjoined her Ascendant in Sagittarius (ruled, of course, by Jupiter). There have been finer singers than Callas, but very few with such a tempestuous lifestyle or such a high profile.

An afflicted Jupiter in this House, however, can lead to a tendency to over-exaggerate and lose one's sense of proportion. Or, again, the effect of Jupiter's expansionary nature in the House of the physical body can lead – as it has in the case of actor Marlon Brando – to an expanding waistline!

An essential part of growing up should be the freedom to explore life without restriction, and to develop one's sense of self-discipline in a relatively carefree environment. However, with Saturn in the First, very often discipline is imposed by outside agencies, blighting personal development and inhibiting spiritual growth.

With a First House Saturn you may be perceived as a reserved and self-contained person; at best, extremely shy and reluctant to reveal the inner you. This is Saturn's protective defence mechanism at work, shielding the persona.

The foundations for your cautious nature were laid in childhood. Looking back at your formative years, you may have felt isolated, or out on a limb, or that the development of your sense of 'self' was denied in some way. Saturn in the First House can indicate a lonely childhood, spiritually if not physically.

Responsibility and obligation come early to the First House Saturn. If Saturn is afflicted by other factors, you may see the world as a cold and harsh place, an unsympathetic arena where you have to struggle in order to establish a sense of identity.

A well-aspected Saturn in the First House can be an asset. It confers self-reliance, dignity, reliability and steadfastness. As a friend, you are as solid as a rock. You are driven by an inherent belief that nothing is easy, and that achievement of any value is only possible by unremitting hard work and discipline.

Uranus represents your individuality and drive for independence. Its position by Sign shows *how* you manifest your unorthodoxy, and its position by House shows *where* you seek to exercise this freedom.

In the First House, Uranus prompts you to seek the freedom to 'be yourself'. Taken to extremes, this can produce eccentricity of character, for you strive to underline the difference between yourself and others. You were odd as a child – exceptionally restless, easily bored, needing constant stimulus and kicking against authority. You expect to go through life untrammelled by the conventions which bind the rest of us.

You're a trail-blazer, disregarding convention and conformity to make your mark on the world in a radically original manner.

Curiously enough, in cases where there is some doubt about an individual's birth time (making it difficult to establish the Rising Sign) it is generally found, upon rectification, that Neptune – the Planet of confusion – is within a few degrees of the Ascendant.

The fundamental principle of Neptune is to dissolve barriers, to negate differences, so that we are all one. And the problem with Neptune in the First House is that the persona is affected by this dissolving quality; the individual falls victim to the process of homogenization. Neptune in the First House may therefore suffer from a life-long lack of self-identity.

Because you have sacrificed your individuality in order to be at one with humanity, you will be perceived as a kind, compassionate, and extremely understanding person. You are very intuitive – even mediumistic or psychic – and are able to 'tune in' to the vibrations around you. Others find you sympathetic and deeply sensitive.

As a child you may have moved in a fantasy world, for deceptive Neptune blurs the edges of reality. This is the Neptune of the Walter Mittys and Billy Liars!

The powerful nature of Pluto, when placed in the First House, intensifies the will and self-awareness of the individual.

Pluto is a ruthless Planet, able to destroy and create, and, in the House of Self, often directs its cathartic energy inwardly. 'If thine eye offend thee, pluck it out', was the advice of St Matthew, and a First House Pluto will use its energy to 'spring-clean' within: to sweep away the old order and give birth to the new; to regenerate. Pluto will spare nothing and no one in order to ensure the survival of the self. The individual with Pluto in the First has the ability and strength to emerge anew from all life's experiences.

As a child, you will have been extremely forceful, determined and intense. Life was a constant battle of wills between you and your parents. You may have been a loner when young (and may remain so now), for other children will have been in awe of you.

Your feelings run deep, and you do not readily – if ever – reveal the 'real' you inside. You are perceived as a strong, silent person, and your air of quiet and controlled power adds to your mystique. As First House Pluto diplomat Henry Kissinger once remarked, 'Power is the ultimate aphrodisiac'.

Paul Newman's Aquarius Sun falls in the First House of his birth chart. Sun in the First is the 'larger than life' placement; it confers vitality and energy and – in this much loved star's case – an overwhelming charisma

THE
SECOND HOUSE

THE HOUSE OF POSSESSIONS

WHEREAS THE FIRST HOUSE was concerned with the individual – the concept of 'Me' – the Second House deals with the individual's possessions and values, and is therefore concerned with the concept of 'Mine'.

From the First House we can derive an idea of your probable physical and psychological structure. We can see the way in which you set about aiming at your life-goals, and the characteristics which were formed during your earliest years.

In other words, the First House shows us the basic skeleton: the Second House will put flesh on the bones.

Linked (by reason of its position in the Natural Zodiac) to the materialistic Sign of Taurus, the function of the Second House is to structure our value system, and to define our resources – to identify what strengths we can call on within ourselves.

We come into life with nothing but a body and a soul. Gradually, as we grow older, we become aware of factors that are personal to us, which are important or of value to us, and which help to shape and define us as individuals. In the Second House, we start to identify and label these factors.

It's rather like taking stock of the food cupboard, or freezer, before a public holiday when the shops are closed. Both are reassuring, displaying what you can draw on, what you have between you and hunger, making you feel secure.

But if there are no labels on the cans or frozen foods, it is impossible to know what sort of meals can be made. Accurate identification of the contents is critical. In the

The function of the Second House is to enable us to define our personal resources, and the strengths we can call on within ourselves. To count our blessings, in fact!

human experience, we look into the Second House for that identification and assessment.

So the Second House is the department where, quite literally, we can 'count our blessings'. Exactly what you value, or take comfort from, is shown by the Sign on the cusp and the celestial bodies that fall within your Second House – your planetary pantry.

Sun in the Second seeks tangible proof of one's importance as an individual. Often this is linked to the acquisition of material possessions or money: a healthy bank balance is a comforting – and visible – validation of one's worth.

The need to amass wealth can drive an individual to power his way from poverty into riches, as with Second House Sun Frank Sinatra, who is not merely a singer, but a substantial businessman (and an incredibly generous person); or Maurice Chevalier, who harnessed the charm of his personality (his Sun) to a minimal talent for singing and dancing, to take him from the slums of his birthplace to Millionaires' Row.

Sun in the Second House confers a high degree of self-reliance. Putting your trust in your own resources avoids the possibility of disappointment in the performance of others: 'If you want a job done properly, do it yourself', is your motto. Your 'security blanket' is the realistic assessment of your life-skills, your assets. You know your strength must come from within.

As well as representing our emotional and feeling nature, the Moon shows our 'maternal' side – how we nurture – and our needs.

Moon in the Second shows the need for a strong value system. In the birth chart of American President George Bush, his Moon conjoins Saturn, the Planet of security and stability. President Bush is no razzmatazz

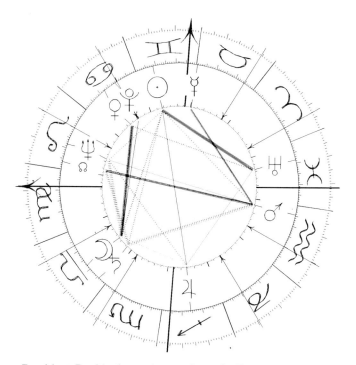

President Bush's chart, shown above, indicates a need for financial stability. Moon in the Second feels insecure when the bank balance is in the red!

politician: he has neither the glamour of Kennedy nor the affability of Reagan. He stands for good old-fashioned values, security, and a well-managed economy. courtesy of his Second House Moon.

In the Second House the Moon reflects its need for emotional security, and is partially comforted and assured by the possession of material resources. Money makes the Moon feel safe in the Second.

The Moon needs to nurture (and be nurtured) in a material sense, too – shelter, warmth, money, clothing and food. You may be no stranger to comfort eating with Moon in the Second! You probably derive a great deal of sensual pleasure from food, and your well-stocked pantry would enable you to survive a prolonged siege.

You are rarely without employment, for you fear financial instability. Your sensitive Moon, though, will generally ensure that you can keep the wolf from the door.

Mercury in the Second can indicate a successful 'wheeler-dealer'. The Planet is shrewd and manipulative and, in the House of Possessions, it can give you the ability to drive a canny bargain.

Mercury is also the Planet of intellect and, in the House of Resources, you may seek intellectual development, for you are fully aware of the value of such improvement and its role in underpinning your earning potential.

In your store cupboard are many cans labelled 'Wit', 'Flexibility', 'Quick Thinking', 'Ingenuity', and 'Communicative Skills'. Mercury in the Second tells you precisely the best time to open them.

With Venus in the Second, there will be no cans of Spam in the store cupboard. This is the pantry of caviar, champagne, *pâté de foie gras* and peaches in brandy, for Venus in the Second gives a love of luxury.

Venus shows us what we find attractive and, in the Second House of Possessions, a great deal of pleasure, comfort and satisfaction is likely to be derived from the ownership of beautiful and valuable items – material assets.

Bestowed by Venus with good taste, 'style' and aesthetic appreciation, you may derive your income from the use of these particular talents in the beauty, fashion or art worlds. You have a fundamental love of money – which is just as well, as you're likely to be extremely extravagant!

If Mars is in the Second House of your chart, you can number amongst your resources assertiveness, initiative, executive action, desire and, above all, energy.

The normal processes of earning money may be too slow for your liking, and you might prefer to be self-employed, or start up a business of your own, so that your abundant energy can be put to good use. You are enterprising and competitive in business.

With this placement, you'll use your aggression and drive to secure and protect your material assets, income and what you hold to be of value.

Jupiter in the Second House has two separate faces. On a materialistic level, possession can spell pleasure, and material success is accorded a high rating on the value scale. Generally, there is 'luck' in business affairs – even relatively risky ones.

On a non-materialistic level, the placement of Jupiter in the Second can bring security and contentment, for the spiritual and philosophical richness of Jupiter's beneficent nature is experienced, and perceived as of immense value.

With Jupiter in the Second, you may have a tendency to profligacy – it's the 'easy come, easy go' placement – but somehow an opportunity always presents itself to bring the bank balance back into credit! Your income may come from the fields of publishing, travel, education or the law.

The function of Saturn is to restrict, delay and deny – not a comfortable prospect when considering your Second House!

There's a great deal of truth in the saying, 'Saturday's child works hard for her living', for the name of the day is a corruption of 'Saturn's Day'.

Saturn in the Second makes you sweat for your money. Material success comes only through a great

Second House Sun Robert De Niro knows that among his major assets he can count on a blazing talent, and highly-bankable acting skills

deal of hard work, and at times the rewards may seem disproportionately small. Frugal and prudent, you are frightened of poverty, and value the protective security of money in the bank.

Possession equates with self-validation, in your eyes, and you may measure your worth against a scale of material ownership.

You should take pride in Saturn's gifts, for Saturn in the Second endows you with ambition, and tempers it with level-headed caution, a healthy dose of realism, and the patience – and the stamina – to achieve success.

With Uranus in the Second, perhaps your greatest personal resource lies in your unorthodoxy. The dictates of convention have no power to bind you to sordid money-grubbing, or to paying lip-service to other people's values. Your free-wheeling nature releases you from the bondage of conformity.

Fine words butter no parsnips, however. There are bills to be paid, obligations to be met, and, with Uranus in the Second House, your finances are subject to wild fluctuation at the best of times.

But the gift of Uranus is originality, even genius. You are possessed of amazing insight, and have a singular talent for spotting potentially beneficial openings.

The erratic nature of Uranus may bring sudden (and radical) destabilizing changes to your financial system. You may lose a fortune, and win it back on the turn of a card.

But Neptune's nature is to dissolve and, let loose in your Second House, you may find that your material resources leach away. This is the House where money simply slips through the fingers, and there may be confusion surrounding your financial situation. Neptune's waters can be muddy in the Second.

The astrological fog which surrounds Neptune may also cloud your value system. Qualities like compassion and empathy may seem too nebulous to be of worth. But, through the mists, we can dimly perceive the ability to heal, a creatively fertile imagination, and a deeply sensitive artistic nature.

To Pluto in the Second House, money means power. It's the power to control. Money, therefore, may be perceived not so much as a trading accessory, but may be vested with great significance, for it can command security, influence, status, respect. He who pays the piper calls the tune.

But not everyone with Pluto in the Second House of Possessions is a mega-tycoon, the Gordon Gecko of the Zodiac. Pluto gives the ability to handle crisis; gives strength and deep perception.

Pluto's ruthless purging quality enables you to strip out the dead wood that may impede and corrupt your progress. Then, uncluttered by life's detritus, you can build your resource bank anew.

Above: Frank Sinatra. He, too, has Sun in the Second House of Possessions and Values

THE
THIRD HOUSE

IN THE FIRST TWO HOUSES, we explored briefly the themes of 'Me' and 'Mine'. In the Third House, we can extend our boundaries to include 'My Territory'.

The Third House is traditionally known as the House of Environment, Communications, Siblings and Education, and – in the Natural Zodiac – it falls in the Sign of Gemini, ruled by Mercury, the Planet whose function is to connect and sequentialize.

The Geminian overtone of the Third House shows how we orient ourselves – how we connect – to the 'outside' generally, and to Third House matters in particular.

The first six Houses of your Horoscope deal with the erection of what will eventually be a sophisticated and complex structure: *you* – a unique entity.

So far, through the First and Second Houses, you have been able to recognize your basic personality, and assess and number your resources. You have begun the process of self-identification as an individual.

The next stage is to see how you view the immediate outside world – the place where you make your initial connections – and how you react to, and interact with, it. It is the first move away from self-absorption.

Perception, or viewpoint, varies from person to person. For example, two children entering infant school together on the first day of term will have totally different impressions of their new environment. To the child plucked from the security of his home and the exclusive and unconditional love of his mother, school may be a frightening place, and education a daunting experience. Another child, who may have mixed in the sociable environment of kindergarten, and be accustomed to sharing

The Third House shows how you make your initial connections, and how you interact with others. It also shows your ability to learn

attention, will see his new school as a boisterous and exciting challenge. The Third House shows how you interpret.

The initial boundary of 'My Territory' is, of course the family and, in particular, brothers and sisters. One's parents are a generation removed but, to a young child, siblings are potential rivals for the limelight, and usurpers of territory. They are a challenge to one's corporeal uniqueness: at the point of establishing a separate identity as an individual comes the alarming realization that there are others sprung from the same source. (Oh, the reassuring comfort of being an 'only'!) The Third House shows the type of relationship you'll enjoy (or not, as the case may be) with your siblings.

Through its link with Mercury, the Planet of intellect, and Gemini, the Sign of communication, your Third House has much to say about your mentality. As you know, the Sign on the cusp of your Third House indicates *how* you process information, and the style in which you communicate (Aries, directly; Libra, fairly; Pisces imaginatively, and so on), and Planets falling in your Third House give an indication of what you think and communicate about.

The Third also shows how you learn. But this is not the higher educational plane of the Ninth House: Education in the Third is more accurately associated with your ability to learn. Knowledge is a great deal more than the mere possession of facts: it is a process whereby information is garnered, and ultimately linked together into concepts. And knowledge is valueless unless it is passed on.

Intellectual capacity is prized when the Sun is in the Third House. You are curious and have a strong drive for knowledge. You want to be seen as clever, and need to be appreciated for your many worthwhile ideas.

You share this placement with a politician and renowned orator. It was said of Winston Churchill that his greatest contribution to the Allied cause was that 'He mobilized the English language.' He spoke from the heart. The power of his Third House Sun mustered British patriotism and rallied the spirit of the nation. 'We shall fight on the beaches,' said Churchill in a stirring call to arms, 'we shall fight on the landing grounds, we shall fight in the fields and in the streets, we shall fight in the hills. We shall never surrender.'

Third House Moon, however, is much more reflective and passive, receiving information and processing it as an emotion. Images from childhood are retained well into adult life, influencing the thought patterns.

This placement appears very commonly in the charts of people in the literary and art worlds – both Michelangelo and Leonardo da Vinci share with you this sensitive position.

The Moon in the Third House of your birth chart indicates an unusually close level of interaction with brothers and sisters. An older sibling may have played the role of 'mother', or this may be a role that you have adopted for yourself. Certainly you feel very protective towards your siblings.

Your retentive memory helped you through your school years, and you appeared a keen student, eager to learn and understand.

As an adult, you may spend a great deal of time daydreaming about your childhood, if it was a happy one, taking out your memories and polishing them one by one, for the comfort and sense of security that you get from remembering happy times.

No Planet is happier in the Third House than Mercury, the ruler of the House in the Natural Zodiac. And, like Mercury, you have a restless, agile mind (and probably

an equally restless, agile lifestyle!)

You are a natural communicator. High telephone bills and long, wordy letters received by your many friends, will attest to this! You are extremely observant and can be very witty. Your mind is teeming with facts and impressions, and you rarely wait to be asked to give your opinion.

As a child you probably learned to read and write quickly and easily, and you may have a flair for foreign languages.

Oscar Wilde, with whom you share this placement, once said, 'We are all in the gutter, but some of us are looking at the stars.' Of course, he may well have been looking at his Third House Mercury.

Venus in the Third endows an intellectual appreciation of literature and the arts.

As a child, you may have spent a great deal of time reading. Splendid tales of heroic exploits, or mythology, were favourite bedtime reading, although as an adult you may prefer light romantic fiction or biographies. You have a gentle way with words, and may have a talent for writing poetry or beautiful love letters.

You may also have a low, melodious voice, and you are a fluent speaker. You are likely to have an inherent sense of language grading, and an instinctive ability to talk in terms of other people's interests.

With Mars in the Third House, you'll display a lively, questing intellect. Sharp-witted, you'll think quickly, and act quickly, too — this is the 'leap before you look' placement.

The Planet of anger and rash action in the House of Communication produces a constant stream of letters signed 'Disgusted, Tunbridge Wells' or 'Angry, of Wisconsin'. And, with your Third House Mars, you may find a great deal of your time is spent in letting off steam over the day-to-day frustrations of normal life. Travel delays, engaged telephone numbers, slow-moving pedestrians, all seem linked in a conspiracy to irritate you. And you are easily irritated, for you are highly strung.

You're a speed freak, too, and probably drive your car far too quickly for safety and/or the speed restrictions in your neighbourhood.

You are likely to experience sibling conflict. This may be because you are challenging a brother or sister for the limelight or supremacy in family status. Reminding yourself of your uniqueness may help to deflate the issue, into the sort of warm and friendly sibling rivalry

With the Sun in this Sign concerned with justice, truth and freedom, and positioned in the Third House of Communication, Winston Churchill's inspirational speeches stiffened the backbone of those fighting the Allied cause in World War Two

as between Shirley MacLaine and her Third House Mars brother, Warren Beatty.

Mars in the Third can be extremely blunt and direct, and consequently extremely rude (albeit inadvertently), so let this Third House Mars author declare that no offence is intended in the statement that Jupiter in the Third generally means a serious case of verbal diarrhoea.

Whatever Jupiter contacts, it inflates and, in your case, Jupiter is expanding your mind: your communicative abilities, your reasoning powers and your intellect. You have much to say: a well-aspected Jupiter will produce many words of wisdom and inspiration; an afflicted Jupiter means windy verbosity and a tendency to exaggeration.

You have a voracious appetite for learning, and a healthy respect for the value of education in general. Intellectual fulfilment comes from enriching your mind. You are quick to grasp the broad outline of any concept.

Jupiter in the Third House can also mean a great deal of travel within your country of residence.

Professor C. E. M. Joad, a panellist on the 'Brains Trust' – a BBC radio forum of the 1940s – gave the British listening public a catchphrase that lingers to this day: 'It all depends on what you mean (by) . . .'. Saturn feels this way too. Saturn in the Third insists on definition and precision. A garden spade is a spade, and not an 'agricultural digging implement'; a church is a church and not a 'religious facility'. This is not the place for 'concepts', but hard facts. Saturn in the Third requires clear and succinct communication, so that the message 'gets across', and no waffle.

At school you may have been a quiet child, slow to learn, and requiring much patience. As a grown-up, you may feel unconfident about your educational attainments, requiring the reassurance of diplomas and certificates – proof of your intellectual achievements. You are likely to be taciturn as an adult, perhaps fearing that you don't have anything much to contribute to everyday chit-chat. However, your opinion is measured and well informed, and generally well respected.

Uranus in the Third produces an original, electric mind that crackles with energy and inventiveness. Others may consider you an 'intellectual revolutionary', for your ideas are radical and ahead of their time. You have practised the principles of freedom of thought and freedom of speech since the day you were born.

Your thought processes do not follow conventional forms, and you can display amazing insight into problems through your ability to think laterally and without bias. Uranus in the Third is frequently the hallmark of genius, and you can congratulate yourself on sharing this placement with Albert Einstein, the physicist who formulated the theory of Relativity.

There may have been frequent changes of schooling

when you were a child, or disruption of some kind in the education process.

You are, incidentally, the only person who can successfully programme the video-recorder!

Neptune in the Third can indicate the 'absent-minded' professor' who seems to operate on a different plane from the rest of us. But it's worth remembering that the 'professor' is only absent-minded because his thoughts

are too focused on higher matters to be concerned with the mundane practicalities of life.

Your Third House Neptune will enable you to absorb impressions by a form of intellectual osmosis: you pick up vibrations, and translate them into sensations and feelings. Because you are so ultra-sensitive, you're able to 'read between the lines' and sense underlying currents of subtle meaning.

This is the Neptune of the day-dreamer. As a child

Like Winston Churchill, Mick Jagger has Sun in the Third, although he's a communicator of a totally different kind

you were frequently chastised for gazing out of the window, moving in a fantasy world of your own making, when you should have been attending to your studies. Your rich and fertile imagination may not have been fully appreciated by your parents, who may have considered you irritatingly vague and dreamy.

'Lacks concentration' frequently appeared on your school reports; school teachers may have considered you not very bright; and you may even have suffered from slight dyslexia. Probably the only teacher to whom you could respond was your English teacher, who inspired you through the medium of books. Science subjects held no appeal at all! Poor pupil you may have been, but you make a superbly inspirational teacher. Because of your sensitive and empathic nature, you can find routes of communication that are not readily apparent to others. You are likely to be extremely artistic.

Pluto in the Third House indicates a deep and penetrative intellect, one that is not content to operate on a superficial level.

You hold very strong opinions and express them forcefully. Many of your ideas are radical in the extreme, and some could be considered harsh. Whilst not denying this, none the less you are able to perceive them as ultimately beneficial, particularly where they affect your local environment.

However, you tend to keep your most private, fundamental, personal thoughts deeply hidden and secretive, unwilling to expose them to public scrutiny. Perhaps sensing your ability to keep your mind open and your lips sealed, friends and neighbours may choose you as a confidante, as a repository for their problems, for you never betray a confidence.

School may have been a not altogether pleasant experience for you, although you are likely to have been a good student, enjoying the investigative nature of research work, and the feeling of power that comes with knowledge.

Light, frivolous, reading is not for you. On your bedside table are many books on the occult, sex manuals, and – of course – detective novels!

Right: Oscar Wilde, who said: 'There is only one thing in the world worse than being talked about, and that is not being talked about.' An apt sentiment for a Third House Mercury!

Opposite: Sir Issac Newton, reputed to have a Third House Sun. When the astronomer, Halley, scorned his interest in astrology, Newton made the rejoinder, 'Sir, I have studied it, you have not.'

THE FOURTH HOUSE

THE HOUSE OF FOUNDATIONS

Your birth chart is divided into four main sections, or quadrants, and these dividing lines are called the 'Angles'.

The Angles are extremely sensitive points. Any Planet touching, or within eight degrees of an Angle, has an enhanced sphere of influence in your Horoscope.

We have already looked at the first Angle (your Ascendant) for it forms the cusp, or beginning, of the First House. The opposite end of the Ascendant is the Descendant, and it marks the beginning of the Seventh House.

But the Angle that completes the division of your chart into quadrants is the MC/IC axis, forming the cusps of the Tenth and Fourth Houses respectively.

The term 'MC' stands for *Medium Coeli* or, in plain English, 'Mid-heaven'. It marks the point of culmination of the Sun, where the Sun is in its highest, or most southerly, position, and corresponds to noon, or midday, on your day of birth.

The opposite point on this axis is the IC, the *Imum Coeli* (literally, the 'undersky'), and it marks the lower meridian on your chart. It corresponds to midnight. The IC forms the cusp of your Fourth House.

The Fourth House is traditionally known as the House of Family and the Home. In actuality, this somewhat inadequate label covers a far wider (and deeper) range of concerns.

Through the first three Houses we have constructed a frame, clothed it and vitalized it. Now – in the Fourth House – it's time to establish it. It's time to put down roots.

The Fourth House has much to say about our origins

The Fourth House – the base of your operations, and where you nurture your 'family'. The place where you hang your hat

and attitude to our background. It shows what we feel about the family unit and our home. Of course, the Sign on the cusp of the Fourth will colour *how* we view the home and family – Sagittarius on the cusp, for instance, may indicate an unwillingness to settle down; Pisces may prefer life afloat!

The Fourth House is indicative not only of our origins, but also of our endings. The Fourth represents conditions we are likely to encounter in the second half of life, after the age of forty. Maturity frequently turns out to be much more fun than youth. We have struggled through the insecurities of adolescence; battled with grim determination through our twenties, establishing careers, homes and families; suffered crises of inadequacy and doubt in our thirties. In our forties, though, having met most of life's eventualities, survived them and established our life principles, there is very little left to do but more of the same, only better.

There is considerable dissent amongst astrologers as to the parental assignment of the Fourth House. Many feel that, because the Fourth in the Natural Zodiac is ruled by the Moon, this House should therefore represent the mother, with the male parent assigned to the Saturnian Tenth House of Prestige and Authority.

Others feel that the Fourth should be assigned to the father – the parent who gives us our name (and nationality) and our genealogical 'line'. In support of this viewpoint, it could be said that maternity is indisputable (and therefore linked to the public aspect of the Tenth), whereas paternity is speculative and perhaps more suitably associated with the 'hidden' nature of the Fourth.

A third school of thought assigns the 'bread-winning' parent to the Tenth, and the 'nurturing' parent to the Fourth. There is no hard and fast rule. Your chart will find a way of telling you, however.

With the Sun in the Fourth House, it is vitally important that you carve a niche for yourself. The keyword is 'establishment'.

You'll have a very strong drive to establish yourself, and may project this dynastic urge on to your family. Like Fourth House Sun Marlon Brando, in his role of of 'The Godfather', you will assume a strongly patrician role. If you have no family of your own, you may take pride in your ancestry, and could develop an interest in genealogy, establishing the line backwards instead of forwards.

It's also important that you establish your own set of traditions; that you create a background, or framework of 'accessories', to put flesh on the bones of your personality; in other words, that you establish evidence of your existence.

It is essential that you establish 'roots'; a home of your own. You need to have a sense of permanence – even with a 999-year lease it seems hardly worth planting the hyacinths. Your home will be highly representative of your character and style, for it represents your powerbase. You may even choose, or prefer, to work from home.

All this may involve you in an arduous uphill struggle during your early years. But, for you, life really does begin at forty. Relaxing in the glow of achievement, you are no longer driven to prove yourself. All you have to establish after forty is the best spot in the garden to put the deckchair!

While Sun in the Fourth beavers away, building his house (humming 'My Way' to himself), Moon in the Fourth prefers the comfort of his familiar stamping-grounds.

The home and family, for you, takes on great emotional significance. Although you may be constantly on the move – your job may take you round the world for months at a time, or you may live in an seemingly endless succession of hotel rooms – there has to be *somewhere* on the face of the earth that you can call 'home'. You must have somewhere to hang your hat. You have a deep-rooted need to belong.

Moon in the Fourth is not emotionally equipped to be an astrological bag-lady. Nor is a home simply a roof to keep the rain off; a shed with carpets. It is a place of sanctuary, where you can take comfort from the secu-

*Typecasting? Fourth House Sun Marlon Brando
in the strongly patriarchial role of Don Vito Corleone in the
film of* The Godfather

rity of your surroundings; a place where you can lick your wounds if need be, and restore yourself.

You probably display many of the 'nurturing' qualities associated with this House: you may be a good amateur (even professional) cook; work in the hotel trade or with property; or act as 'mother hen' to your employees, treating them all as one big family. You are a kind and thoughtful person.

With Mercury in the Fourth, there is a strong possibility that you will come from an academic background, or a large, bookish family.

If you have children of your own, you are probably keen to encourage their literary pursuits, and are a staunch advocate of the bedtime story routine. Family gatherings probably include games of charades, quizzes or Trivial Pursuit tournaments. Card games, naturally, include Happy Families!

Your home is likely to be full of people at all hours of the day and night – family, friends and neighbours who seem to come and go as they please, and who may cause you to wonder at times: am I running a home or a hotel?

With the second half of life being emphasized by this House, it is entirely possible that, once your family has grown up and become reasonably independent, you may re-enter the educational system as a mature student, or undertake retraining in some skill or vocation.

Gentle Venus ensures a warm welcome for anyone who crosses over your threshold, for your home is probably the most comfortable in the entire Zodiac.

Battling children, warring grown-ups, discordant music from the stereo, or blaring TV in every room are unlikely to be found behind your front door. Venus in the Fourth House strives for peaceful harmony and smooth relationships within the family unit. The family is close and happily integrated, and very affectionate.

You are probably a good home-maker, with a love of cooking and entertaining. You have impeccable taste, and your home is likely to be pleasantly furnished and decorated.

Your interests may well extend to the garden, too, for you love to fill your home with beautiful flowers. And if you're a Fourth House Venus on the eighteenth floor of an apartment-block, you'll have the best window-boxes in town.

Mars in the Fourth brings its aggression home every time it walks through the door.

Aggression doesn't have to equate with hostility or anger, of course – there is no implication that, at the end of the day, you come home and sock your partner on the jaw, or biff a child round the ears – but you certainly express your drive and energy inside the four walls of your home.

Like a battery left on charge overnight, your Martian traits are activated and stimulated by the home environment. This could lead to a mania for DIY, for instance, where every weekend is spent up a ladder, and the house reverberates to the merry sound of hammering.

Your Mars competitiveness has to find an outlet and, in the Fourth, is likely to be expended on your children as well as the home. You'll enthusiastically encourage them in their sports and activities, and urge them to succeed. You may be the wrong age (or the wrong shape) for puffing round a football pitch yourself, but you can certainly cheer from the sidelines.

Expansive Jupiter in the Fourth can often indicate a large family and a large home to accommodate it. But, whatever the actual size of your home – and irrespective of whether it's a mansion, a suburban semi, or a canvas tent halfway up a Himalayan mountain – it will be imbued with love, warm affection, comfort and security. (Wow! Let's all move to your house!)

Spiritual values and a strong sense of morality will be found under the Jupiterian roof. The family is close-knit and will generally hold an enviable position within the community. 'Good family' is the name of the game when Jupiter is in the Fourth.

Life mellows in maturity. You can afford to sit back and put your feet up, confident in the knowledge that the 'luck' that comes your way is simply a just reward for a job well done and a life well lived.

Saturn in the Fourth can sometimes bring a sense of insecurity to childhood, leaving a scar that may take years to fade.

Your early years were probably neither very happy

Neptune requires a sacrifice. HRH The Duke of Windsor sacrificed his home, family and his heritage for the sake of the woman he loved

'Family' is all-important to Fourth House Sun Michael Jackson, whether comprised of blood relations, his musical entourage or his menagerie of animals

nor very easy ones. Finances may have been difficult, or family circumstances crushingly burdensome. Duty or responsibility may have combined to isolate you from your peers. Somewhere along the line, the familial support and nurture that is the birthright of every child was missing. Saturn in the Fourth hoes a lonely row as a child.

Your deep-seated fear that the pattern might be repeated is not without its positive side, however, and you have grown up strongly self-reliant and determined to make a secure base for your own family. You have learned how to generate your own emotional strength within, rather than relying on its coming from without. Stability, security, and rock-solid foundations are Saturn's old-age gifts to those who have learned their lessons well.

Uranus in the Fourth can indicate an unsettled home life. This is the stateless person, the refugee of the Zodiac, who never really feels at home anywhere.

If Uranus is in the fourth sector of your chart, there was probably much domestic disruption when you were younger – uprootings, 'moonlight flits', changes of residence because of family circumstances or a parental career. You may have left home at an early age to travel, or live in a commune, or among like-minded people, and may eventually settle in a country or city far from your place of birth.

You tend to view your family in a detached light, seeing them as a collection of interesting people housed under the same roof, unvested with the emotionally close bonds of kinship. Neither is your home of any great sentimental significance, and Uranus enables you to pack up and move to a new location with scarcely a backward glance.

Often, when Neptune is found in the Fourth House, it demands a sacrifice. The Duke of Windsor (formerly King Edward VIII), who shares this placement with you, relinquished his rights to the throne, gave up his family and his heritage, and went into exile from his country – the price he had to pay for marrying the woman he loved.

Such a drastic sacrifice is not demanded of us all. In your case, you may have had to give up exclusive rights to your bedroom, for instance, in order that the family could accommodate a foster-child. Perhaps a sick or disabled sibling took the lion's share of parental attention in your family. You may even have been institutionalized for part of your childhood. These early experiences have left you with a deeply compassionate and self-sacrificing nature.

With Neptune, the Planet of idealism, in the Fourth House, there is a tendency to look back on childhood years as the 'good old days', when summers were hot and sunny, winters were crisp with snow, Sundays were redolent of the smell of apple pie, and life was full of laughter.

Harry Belafonte, another Fourth House Neptune, sang his happy perception of his Jamaican home in the famous song 'Island in the Sun', recalling its coral sands, clear shining waters, and perpetual sunshine.

But Neptune has a very selective memory, and soon forgets the wasp stings of summer, the chilblains of win-

ter, the family fights over washing up the Sunday dishes, and overlooks the jellyfish and the sandflies of Belafonte's idealized version of his childhood home. (To be fair, the song would never have got into the charts if it had not!)

Growing up for a Fourth House Pluto may have been a more than usually scary process. Dark undercurrents may have swirled around the whole issue of childhood: crisis, a family secret or the painful disintegration of the family unit, may have melded together to form a picture of Hogarthian misery, to a child's eyes. But whereas

Saturn in the Fourth would interpret this as bleak but unavoidable, Pluto sees it as unacceptable, and has the strength to tear it down and destroy it, in order to start again.

With the regenerative force of Pluto in the Fourth House of your chart, you may have had to make irrevocable and painful decisions, as an adult, in order to gain control of your domestic life and environment. It's made you strong, though, and capable: it's made you a survivor. And, although it would be unfair to call you a domestic despot, there's absolutely no doubt who wears the trousers in your household!

THE
FIFTH HOUSE

THE HOUSE OF CREATIVITY

Constructed, furnished, vitalized and domiciled, we can now afford to 'take five' (appropriately enough) and explore the 'Saturday Night' section of your chart.

The Fifth House is traditionally understood to show how we enjoy ourselves, what we find pleasurable, and is also concerned with love affairs, creativity and children (these are often causally linked, it must be said!).

But an inability to sing, dance, paint or make music, or display any tangible creative talent, does not condemn us astrologically. We needn't necessarily feel a failure if we take no pleasure from the making of raffia baskets, nor should we feel unfulfilled if we are childless or celibate.

For 'creativity' read 'importance'. For by far the greatest function of the Fifth House is to demonstrate the way in which you are special. In this respect, the Fifth House serves to underline our uniqueness.

Sun in the Fifth is 'Mr (or Ms) Entertainment', for this is the natural home of the Sun and the place where it loves to shine.

A Fifth House Sun goes through life to the fanfare of trumpets, and under a perpetual spotlight, for this is the placement of blazing talent and precocity.

Scientist, engineer and artist Leonardo da Vinci (who, between painting *The Last Supper* and the *Mona Lisa* in the fifteenth century, also found time to design a flying machine), and Mozart (who composed over 600 musical works in his thirty-five years of life) both share this aspect of your chart. So does razzle-dazzler

It's love that makes the world go round, it's said.
The Fifth House has much to say about love affairs and the
style of your personal creativity

Liberace; child prodigy Shirley Temple; and the flamboyant Zsa Zsa Gabor. A Fifth House Sun is no astrological wallflower.

The first thing that must be said about you is that you have tremendous *joie de vivre*; you are determined to get as much as you possibly can from life, and to live it to the full. You feel good when you're the centre of attention, surrounded by your many adoring friends.

You love to be in love, and revel in the trappings of romance. You give love whole-heartedly and with great gusto. Even standing in your shadow is like basking in the sunshine.

You may feel you're not conventionally creative, but a Sun in the Fifth totally devoid of talent has yet to be born. And even if it's 'only' the ability to make other people feel special, it's a gift for which a kingship and a crown were once abandoned. (Wallis Simpson had Sun in the Fifth.)

Because the Moon symbolizes the mother, and the Fifth House is concerned with children, you are likely to experience a deeply engrained need to have children of your own. Furthermore, this placement usually indicates fecundity.

The emotional nature of the Moon adds a further dimension. Happy memories of your childhood could spur you to re-create them, through procreation, for the next generation; to 'turn the clock back'.

You are naturally talented and artistic, and you probably express this through painting or drawing.

You are generally well liked by all those who come into contact with you, for you have the gift of reflecting back to them, in generous measure, what it pleases them to hear. In love, you seek an emotionally supportive partner who understands your needs and your sensitive, caring nature.

Creativity, when Mercury is in the Fifth House, is often expressed through the medium of the spoken and written word, and you may therefore have a flair for writing. A good outlet for your talents might be in public relations, or you could make an effective teacher, for you have the happy knack of making the learning process stimulating and a lot of fun.

You are bright and lively, with a fertile, active brain. Relaxation takes the form of games of skill and strategy, such as chess.

Wit and mental agility are essential qualities in a love partner, who should also be capable of appreciating your own substantial intellect!

Venus in the Fifth House imparts a warm and loving glow to your personality, and makes you one of the most popular members of the Zodiac.

Right: A Fifth House Sun, like Shirley Temple, adores being the centre of attention

Below: Child prodigy, Wolfgang Amadeus Mozart had the Sun (will), Mercury (communication) and Saturn (discipline) in the Fifth House

You're nothing but a big kid at heart, who loves to play and give pleasure. It may interest you to know that Walt Disney, who created Mickey Mouse, also had Venus in the Fifth.

You'll encourage your children in their creative pursuits and derive as much pleasure from their achievements as they do.

In love you're the arch-Romantic. *Affaires* are vitally important to your sense of well-being, for you love the sensation of being loved.

Couple the House of Leisure, Love and Creativity with the Planet of lust, passion and sex appeal, and what do

you think we get? We get *Playboy* Hugh Hefner, that's who!

You may not be in the Hefner league (for his Fifth House Mars conjoins Jupiter, the Planet that does everything on a big scale), but you'll certainly be in a class of your own when it comes to love.

Love equates with passion in your book. You love madly, aggressively, ardently and with great urgency. A badly aspected Mars will love jealously.

Mars works hard and, in this House, plays hard. Relaxation normally takes the form of strenuous and competitive sport where you can sweat out your natural aggression. However, Mars in the Fifth House finds little difference between the squash court and the bedroom, and consequently spends a great deal of time 'horizontally jogging'!

In this House, Jupiter enhances the creative capacity. Artistic hobbies may grow into extremely satisfying full-time interests.

Children respond well to you, and look to you for guidance. You would make an excellent Scout leader, or counsellor at summer camp.

Jupiter in the Fifth has an immense capacity for enjoyment, and a tremendous appetite for pleasure – the riskier the better.

Bruce Springsteen's packed Fifth House (Sun, Moon, Venus and Neptune) indicates a wealth of creative talent

Since risk-taking and gambling come under the umbrella of the Fifth House, and Jupiter has rulership over horses, Jupiter in the Fifth is the bookies' favourite punter. You're game for a flutter, whether it's on the racecourse, at the casino or on the Stock Market. (You tend to gamble in love, too.) Unfortunately, however, Jupiter's breezy confidence may encourage you to turn a blind eye to the possibility of losing, and you may speculate unwisely. 'Ah well,' says Jupiter with a shrug of the shoulders, 'easy come; easy go.'

Saturn in the Fifth takes its pleasures seriously. The inhibiting nature of Saturn can be an astrological wet-blanket in the House of Pleasure. However frivolous and silly you'd like to be, there's always a still small voice inside saying, 'Now, hold on a minute.'

A heavy burden of duty and responsibility as a child may have inhibited your capacity for frivolity. A Fifth House Saturn always has to do the dishes first.

This caution and reserve can also hamper your romantic prospects. You may not voice your love until you feel the time is right, or you may be unwilling to dive headfirst into the unrestrained waters of love's swimming-pool.

Having children of your own may be delayed until later in life, or denied altogether. Your family, if you have one at all, is likely to be small.

Because Saturn insists on hearing the bad news first, let's look now at the positive aspect of this placement.

You are able to impose a sense of structure on your creative expression. With Saturn in the Fifth you won't be lounging about the house, strumming on a guitar and dreaming of glory; you'll be out there organizing gigs and licking the band into shape. You would make an ideal manager in the entertainment world.

Romantically, you may find fulfilment with an older, more mature person later in life. And all good things are worth waiting for.

The combination of the Fifth House of Creativity and the eccentricity of Uranus can have an electrifying (and sometimes shocking) effect on artistic expression. For instance, it gave us Elvis Presley, who so offended our sensibilities in the 1950s by performing in a strange new musical style to the accompaniment of overtly sexual grindings of his pelvis, that television companies were obliged to film him only from the waist up.

With this placement, you are likely to develop wild enthusiasms for unconventional hobbies and pleasures. Easily bored, you'll switch your interests at the drop of a hat, seeking constant stimulus and excitement.

Love affairs, too, may be erratic, and you'll be drawn to unconventional types who share your enjoyment of the unusual.

Creative expression is greatly enhanced by the presence of Uranus in the Fifth, particularly in the fields of electronic art and television.

Neptune is associated with escapism – how we transcend reality. We may either escape upwards (Neptune has a refining and purifying effect) towards perfection, or we may sink into oblivion in muddy, murky waters of drugs and alcohol. No coincidence, then, that Fifth House Neptune Dean Martin is rarely seen expressing his creativity without a glass of Scotch in his hand!

Creative expression, for you, may have involved you in some sort of sacrifice in your early years. Perhaps piano lessons may have had to be abandoned because of family finances. Or perhaps the needs of your children have required the martyrdom of your own talent.

Someone who shares this placement with you is Bruce Springsteen, a performer whose talent – like Neptune itself – knows no bounds.

Pluto is incapable of doing anything by halves. It brings a level of intensity to all Fifth House matters – love, pleasure and creativity.

Falling in love, for a Fifth House Pluto, can be a regenerative experience. You may feel cleansed, reborn and spiritually renewed, but the strength of your feelings may lead to a power complex, where you have to be the dominant and conquesting partner.

Creative expression for you is not a light-hearted matter, and may involve issues from your subconscious that have percolated to the surface.

Because of Pluto's regenerative nature, your ideal form of relaxation is probably a car boot sale!

No one could call Zsa Zsa Gabor an astrological wallflower! Her Fifth House Sun ensures her gift for publicity and her high profile often outshine her talent for acting

ATTRACTION POTENTIAL

	ARIES	TAURUS	GEMINI	CANCER	LEO	VIRGO
ARIES	Both want to be 'No. 1'. Self-ishness intrudes — 1	Satisfying, if an effort is made — 2	Sparky and fizzy, but no substance — 1	Potentially emotionally explosive — 3	Five-star unhibited passion — 5	This works better as a friendship — 1
TAURUS	Conflicting needs, but basically strong — 2	Mutually indulgent and easy-going — 1	He's too restless for her. No real rapport — 1	Warm and feeling relationship — 3	Mutual devotion, pride, and stubborness — 1	Earthy and sensual. Mutual respect — 3
GEMINI	Needs variety to stimulate the relationship — 2	Out of step with each other — 1	Too much love-talk; too little action! — 3	He may dampen her enthusiasm. Affectionate — 1	Demands and compromises – but fun — 2	Irritating differences may spoil this — 1
CANCER	Damp matches strike no sparks — 1	Deeply affectionate — 3	Imaginative — 1	Concealed feelings — 3	She needs more TLC than he can give — 1	Understanding affinity — 2
LEO	Hot love but rivalry for the spotlight — 2	Both too stubborn, but very sensual — 1	Bright and easy. May lack substance — 2	She needs ador-ation; he needs reassurance. — 1	Together they'll conquer the world — 3	Considerate and enthusiastic — 2
VIRGO	One-sided. Too demanding — 1	Refined relationship, but earthy loving — 3	Clash of temperaments — 1	Muddy waters — 1	Controlled excitement — 3	Far too critical — 2
LIBRA	Mutual rapport. Could lack warmth — 2	Subtly erotic — 2	A fusion of intellects — 5	She may inhibit him — 1	Extremely promising! — 3	Handle with care — 1
SCORPIO	Ardent emotions. Sexy! — 3	Intensely possessive — 3	Like ill-fitting shoes — 1	Both need reassurance and privacy — 3	Stubbornness. Requires adjustment — 2	Tamped-down and controlled emotions — 1
SAGITTARIUS	Fun, but he's too self-centred — 2	Different needs and natures — 1	Lacking constancy — 1	He can't handle her mind games — 1	A pair of crazy kids — 3	Edgy — 1
CAPRICORN	Good solid working relationship — 2	Ambitious intentions. Quiet loving — 3	Mildly frustrating — 1	She may lack empathy — 1	Enduring affections — 2	Very strong loving. Understanding — 5
AQUARIUS	Irritating. He's bossy; she's obstinate — 1	Too much of a challenge — 1	Airborne delights — 3	She's too detached for him — 1	Challenging fun — 3	Pleasurable, but remote — 1
PISCES	Great intensity and imagination — 3	Desires blend well — 2	Erratic needs — 1	Closely attuned — 5	He demands too much — 1	Natural empathy — 3

To assess the potential for compatibility between two people, all ten Planets (and the Houses they fall into) in each person's chart must be compared and considered. However, this Sun Sign comparison table will indicate likely basic attractions - the complicated stuff can come later! For male signs, read from the top; for female signs, read from the left. A score of five indicates great compatibility

LIBRA	SCORPIO	SAGITTARIUS	CAPRICORN	AQUARIUS	PISCES	
His mood swings make her impatient (3)	Deep and meaningful; jealousy possible (2)	Crazy, irresponsible fun (3)	He may dampen her enthusiasm. Different goals (2)	Pleasant, if detached, relationship (1)	Unrealistic living, but 'fairy-tale' loving (1)	ARIES
Many shared interests. Loving (2)	Powerful and intense but possessive (3)	She needs someone more stable (1)	Loving security ensures happiness (5)	Poles apart. Both march to different drums (1)	Lazy, comfortable love (2)	TAURUS
A meeting of minds. Mental poetry (5)	Could be well-suited (2)	Inspired bedroom games! (3)	Comforting. He's supportive, she's refreshing (2)	Free-spirited friendship (3)	He's too slippery for her (1)	GEMINI
Could be satisfying (2)	Passionate fulfilment (5)	Inexplicable attraction (2)	Serious and caring (2)	Lacking in mutual humour (1)	Soothing and gentle (3)	CANCER
Mellow and romantic (2)	Blows hot and cold. Both stubborn (3)	Wild and wonderful loving (5)	Given time, it may work (2)	Crazy love – many arguments (3)	Unlikely to work. Tolerance needed. (1)	LEO
Peaceful and co-operative (2)	He's too much for her to handle (1)	Could be emotionally bruising (1)	Slow sensuality (5)	He'll lighten her up (2)	Emotional release experienced (3)	VIRGO
Rarely dull (2)	Ecstasy possible – with luck! (2)	She can't tie him down (1)	Cool, but friendly co-operation (2)	Light and breezy (3)	Dreamy (2)	LIBRA
Out of tune (1)	Unfathomably deep (3)	Too tense (1)	Safe and uncomplicated (2)	Physical bond is weak (1)	The emotional ultimate! (5)	SCORPIO
Open, fair and sharing (2)	Drowned by his emotions (1)	Free and easy loving. Same goals (5)	He robs her of confidence (1)	Friendly and generous (3)	Effort is needed (1)	SAGITTARIUS
He's too cool for her (2)	A pair of stick-in-the-muds (2)	Lighten up lady, or lose him (1)	Initially, love is cautious – but close (2)	Hard to settle (1)	He makes her her feel so young (2)	CAPRICORN
Physically calm, but mentally stimulating (3)	Conflict likely (1)	Capricious but affectionate (2)	She's too unpredictable (1)	Off the wall! (5)	She moves too quickly for him (1)	AQUARIUS
Mutually considerate (2)	Wonderful depths (3)	Lacks consideration (1)	Practical combination (2)	She's too dreamy for him (1)	Soul mates (3)	PISCES

THE SIXTH HOUSE

THE HOUSE OF SERVICE

In Part One of this book we made an analogy between a birth chart and an architectural blueprint, pointing out that in the same way that a blueprint shows the envisaged design, size and purpose of a building under construction, a birth chart shows the potential of an individual.

So far the astrological blueprint has given us an indication of your likely character, the resources available to you and your type of outlook. It has also indicated the sort of base from which you operate, and the way in which you make your individual mark upon the world. Like the pieces in an astrological jigsaw puzzle, the different sectors of your Horoscope are slowly building up into a picture.

But now it's time to pause and take stock. It's time for a 'site meeting', in fact; time to reappraise what's taking shape under the scaffolding; time to look objectively at the first five storeys; time for the architect to advise us on the necessity for modifications to the blueprint. Time, in fact, to go to the Sixth House.

A major function of the Sixth House is to enable us to recognize the link between understanding and doing. This is the handiwork of Mercury. In the Natural Zodiac, the Sixth House corresponds to Virgo, ruled by Mercury, and this lively Planet links the mentality of Gemini (also ruled by Mercury) – 'understanding' – with the Earthy practicality of Virgo – 'doing'. For the acquisition of skill comes not from blindly imitating an action on a 'monkey see, monkey do' basis, but from understanding how the action is reproduced and what is required for this.

The Sixth House is where we roll up our sleeves, and get on with the job. It is a House of Duty and Service

It is not enough for a musician to seat himself at the piano, with a soulful expression on his face, and bang the keys at random in a parody of playing (although we've all heard piano recitals where it seems that something of this nature is taking place): he has to learn the process of making the link whereby notes on a page of music can be translated into movements of the fingers.

Health is another department firmly under the domain of the Sixth House, which operates a strict policy of *mens sana in corpore sano*. In this respect, the Sixth House can be likened to an astrological engineer, who ensures that the machine is kept in good working order. The Sixth House is responsible for our inner discipline: the machine that's well maintained performs better and more reliably.

'After the parade comes the dustcart', it's said, and the Sixth House is where we enter dustcart territory. For the dustcart is an essential (albeit unseen and unsung) part of the razzmatazz of the big parade. Without it, the streets would be knee-deep in tickertape, and the city awash with litter. Without the 'essential dustcart' of the Sixth House, the potential of the first five Houses would be wasted. For the primary function of the Sixth is to assess what must be done in order to make use of the astrological components delineated and described by the first five Houses.

The Sixth House is particularly concerned with adjustment to necessity. Corresponding to the Sign of Virgo in the Natural Zodiac, it is an eminently practical House, and never shirks its duty. It peers over the shoulder of the Fifth and dishes out down-to-earth, realistic advice on how to develop its talents. 'Excuse me, but how do I get to Carnegie Hall?' asks the bewildered tourist, lost on a sight-seeing trip. 'Practise, lady. You gotta practise,' sighs the Sixth House New Yorker resignedly.

In this respect, then, the Sixth House is where we recognize and acknowledge what needs to be done, and where we learn to improve – through practice, hard work and the application of common sense and practicality – all that we have so far achieved.

With his Cardinal Libra Sun and Mars conjoined in the House of Duty, John Lennon (above) provided the driving force, and the backbone, of the Beatles. His birth chart (below) shows his immense capacity for hard work

Sun in the Sixth expresses its individuality and life force through service – through doing the best possible job. If your Sun is in this House, you have every right to take pride in the work you do. You're a 'detail' person, systematic, organized, and highly efficient, concerned with the smooth running of daily life.

You are fully aware of the value of your contribution to society and expect to be remunerated accordingly (after all, the labourer is worthy of the hire) and to be respected for what you do. Your role may not be ultra-glamorous, but it's utterly essential.

You share this placement with John Lennon. The iron discipline of his Sixth House Sun kept him practising the guitar until his fingers bled, while he developed and improved his Fifth House talents in defiance of his Aunt Mimi's daily put-down: 'Playing the guitar's all right for a hobby, John, but you'll never make a living out of it!'

An interesting example of Moon in the Sixth is provided by the chart of Marie Stopes, who outraged Victorian society at the beginning of the century with her pioneering work bringing contraception and family planning to the working classes, in an effort to stem the rising tide of infant (and maternal) mortality, and to improve health standards. With empathetic and compassionate Pisces on the cusp of her Sixth House, her Moon (aptly representing motherhood as well as the public) was strongly aspected by Uranus, the radical Planet that likes to shock. Incidentally, her Ascendant was in the practical and health-oriented Sign of Virgo, the natural ruler of the Sixth.

The Moon seeks security and reassurance wherever it finds itself in a chart and, in the Sixth, consoles itself with a stable routine and comforting rituals.

You may change employment frequently. Job satisfaction is more easily obtained when you work with other people with whom you can interact, or where you can meet the public.

Because of the fluctuating nature of the Moon, and the consequent effect it has on the emotions, this placement may produce a higher than usual interest in the maintainance of good health. A badly aspected Moon, however, could indicate a degree of hypochondria or psychosomatic illness.

Emotional disturbance can lead to dietary disorder, and you should guard against anorexa nervosa or bulimia by avoiding 'comfort eating' or food binges. You must establish a well-balanced nutritional programme.

For you, a good way to maintain your equilibrium, and to provide an essential sense of routine, is to welcome a cat or a dog into your life. A small creature to love – and who will love you back – will be a comfort to your soft and gentle (and somewhat fragile) Moon.

Opposite: Sixth House Sun Alfred Hitchcock on the set of The Birds

This House traditionally includes attitudes to health regimes, and to household pets and small creatures

Mercury in the Sixth is the specialist of the Zodiac. With this placement, you're keen to acquire knowledge and skill, and to find out exactly how things work. You need to keep busy all the time.

'If a job's worth doing, it's worth doing well', says Venus in the Sixth, who carries out every function – however mundane, however dull – perfectly. You'll put as much effort into (and get almost as much enjoyment out of) cleaning the bathroom as you do icing a cake.

Energetic Mars works hard in the Sixth, particularly at jobs requiring precision or mechanical ability. (With Mars in this House, though, you need to guard against the possibility of injury from sharp tools or machinery.) You might do well as a trade union leader.

Jupiter usually seeks to do 'good works' in the Sixth. With this placement, a great deal of satisfaction is obtained from knowing that you have been of practical service. Your daily work could involve sport, travel or teaching.

Saturn in the Sixth generally means a great deal of very hard work and attention to detail. You take your responsibilities seriously and have a cautious approach to your work.

Uranus brings a touch of unorthodoxy to daily matters and routine work. You may develop new techniques at the work-place, or have an 'alternative' approach to health.

The Sixth is not the ideal place for Neptune. You may find it hard to discipline yourself to work, and may experience periods of unemployment. However, this placement can also mean that you may have the gift of healing.

Pluto in the Sixth gives you the will to improve your working conditions by making sweeping changes. A job involving the recycling of resources would suit you well, as would any kind of investigative work, or the nuclear energy industry, or work in a hospice.

THE SIXTH HOUSE AND HEALTH

The Sixth House is where we look for specific references to health. Each of the Signs of the Zodiac is associated with a part of the body, and each Sign is ruled by a Planet which itself rules a part of the body.

To discover your astrological 'weak spot', check the Sign on the cusp (the beginning) of your Sixth House,

and compare it with the table below.

However, if you don't know your time of birth, you will be unable to ascertain your Ascendant and, without an Ascendant, you cannot accurately determine the Sign on your Sixth House cusp.

In that event, ask your local astrologer to prepare you a Solar chart. This will assume your Ascendant to be at the same degree of the Zodiac as your Sun, and the Houses will be numbered accordingly.

Therefore, with a Solar chart, if your 'Ascendant' is in the Sign of:

ARIES your 'Sixth House' will be in VIRGO
TAURUS your 'Sixth House' will be in LIBRA
GEMINI your 'Sixth House' will be in SCORPIO
CANCER your 'Sixth House' will be in SAGITTARIUS.
LEO your 'Sixth House' will be in CAPRICORN
VIRGO your 'Sixth House' will be in AQUARIUS
LIBRA your 'Sixth House' will be in PISCES
SCORPIO your 'Sixth House' will be in ARIES
SAGITTARIUS your 'Sixth House' will be in TAURUS
CAPRICORN your 'Sixth House' will be in GEMINI
AQUARIUS your 'Sixth House' will be in CANCER
PISCES your 'Sixth House' will be in LEO

Once you have determined the Sign on the cusp of the Sixth House, you can easily identify the corresponding part of the body. However, it should be stressed that the conditions described under 'May manifest as . . .' do not mean you will necessarily experience a health problem in the relevant area. And, of course, it cannot be too heavily emphasized that there is absolutely *no* connection between the Sign of Cancer and the malignancy of the same name.

ARIES on the Sixth House cusp:
    The head; the brain; the muscular tissues; the nose; the adrenal gland.
    May manifest as: headaches; migraines; fevers; nervous attacks; head injuries.

TAURUS on the Sixth House cusp:
    The neck; the throat; the thyroid gland.
    May manifest as: tonsillitis; poor metabolism (and consequent weight gain).

GEMINI on the Sixth House cusp:
    The lungs; arms; hands; the nervous system.
    May manifest as: chest infections; nervous attacks

CANCER on the Sixth House cusp:
    The breasts; the stomach; the ovaries and uterus; the lymph glands.
    May manifest as: menstrual problems.

LEO on the Sixth House cusp:
    The heart; the spine.
    May manifest as: circulatory problems.

VIRGO on the Sixth House cusp:
    The intestines.
    May manifest as: gastritis; nervous indigestion.

LIBRA on the Sixth House cusp:
    The kidneys.
    May manifest as: kidney stones; chronic backache; urological problems.

SCORPIO on the Sixth House cusp:
    The reproductive system; the genitals.
    May manifest as: uro-genital problems; constipation.

SAGITTARIUS on the Sixth House cusp:
    The thighs; the hips; the liver.
    May manifest as: pelvic disorders; jaundice.

CAPRICORN on the Sixth House cusp:
    The bones (particularly the knees); the teeth; the spleen.
    May manifest as: osteo-arthritis; cartilage problems.

AQUARIUS on the Sixth House cusp:
    The calves; the ankles.

PISCES on the Sixth House cusp:
    The feet; the pineal gland.

THE
SEVENTH HOUSE

THE HOUSE OF PARTNERSHIPS

The second half of a horoscope can be said to be a 'higher octave' of the first six Houses. For instance, in the First House we met the self, but in the Seventh we meet the self in relation to others. In the Second House we looked at personal resources; in the Eighth we turn to shared resources. In the Third House, mentality; in the Ninth, the higher mind. And so on.

Hopefully, the journey we have taken through the first six Houses will have established your personality. We have identified six separate stages of development – physical structure, assets, mentality, foundations, creative spark and realistic practicality – and seen how they combine to make the individual which you undoubtedly are. You may consider yourself complete.

But no man is an island, as the poet John Donne wrote some 300 years ago. And never were truer words uttered. We cannot exist in a vacuum, for each one of us is part of the interdependent, interactive structure of life. If each one of us has something to give (and we *all* have something to contribute), then it follows that there must be someone to receive.

We are now moving into the realms of the Seventh House. Traditionally described as the House of Partnerships, it is the place where we meet others on a one-to-one basis.

The term 'partnerships' does not apply exclusively to romantic partnerships (although these are of primary significance). 'Partners' in the Seventh means people with whom we have a relationship of some kind.

The cusp of the Seventh House – the Descendant – is a particularly sensitive part of a Horoscope, for it is one of

The nature and quality of one-to-one relationships is shown by the Seventh House. It is where we meet our 'significant others'

the four Angles, and the counterpart of the Ascendant. If the Ascendant focuses on the self as a separate entity, the Descendant focuses on the involvement of the self with others.

The ruler of the Seventh House in the Natural Zodiac is, of course, Venus. This Planet's function is to attract, to socialize, to make relationships and to harmonize. Falling in love is the relationship that most obviously springs to mind in the context of the Seventh House!

The quality of our relationships, and how we relate, is shown by the Seventh House. It corresponds, in the Natural Zodiac, to the Sign of Libra (represented by The Scales), and Libra's function is to strive for balance.

Does this mean, then, that falling in love is nothing more than a convenient arrangement for balancing the scales? That the beloved is simply a 'make-weight' — someone to counteract our own deficiencies and make up the shortfall? Someone whose sole purpose is to contribute the qualities we feel we lack, or have in short supply, in order to make a balanced partnership?

Of course not. Someone, somewhere, once said, 'Love consists of this: that two solitudes reach out, and greet, and comfort one another', and this is what we do in the Seventh House. We give. We contribute. The joint contributions of two individuals, complete in themselves, create a third entity: a relationship. The total becomes greater than the sum of the parts. For the secret of compatibility in a love relationship lies not in the duplication of emotions, but in the existence of complementary feelings.

What do we want from a marriage or love partner? The Seventh House will tell us.

'Relating' is the name of the game for Sun in the Seventh. Somehow you seem to express yourself more completely, and find a greater degree of self-validation, through the medium of a partner. Relating to another person brings out your unique qualities and helps shape your identity by giving you a sense of perspective. Through partnership you can blossom.

You share this placement with Warren Beatty and Omar Sharif, both of whom are as famous for their romantic involvements as for their acting! Another Seventh House Sun is Sean Connery, whose screen roles have so often revolved around the 'relating' principle – particularly in his highly successful series of 'James Bond' films.

But a Seventh House Sun is not all sweetness and light, for you also share this placement with Adolf Hitler. Hitler's Sun conjoined his Mercury, and both Planets were placed on the Descendant, the cusp of the house where we meet the 'not-self'; the 'significant other'.

Hitler's 'significant others' were the members of the National Socialist Party. His gifts as an orator (Jupiter/Moon conjunction in the Third) enabled him to play skilfully on the emotions of the masses, and a forceful combination of his personality/will (the Sun) and his communicative abilities (Mercury) in the Seventh, allowed his absolute and untrammelled rise to power.

On an altogether different note, perhaps the world's best-loved Seventh House Sun is Diana, Princess of Wales. Marriage did not change her personality, but it certainly changed her status. Two words –'I will' – changed her from a nursery school teacher to a celebrity, and from a minor aristocrat to a Princess, the third most important lady in the land. Marriage, for Diana, allowed her Sun to shine.

Moon in the Seventh brings its sensitive and reflective nature to the House of Partnerships. On the face of it, it might seem that the Seventh House is an excellent place for the Moon, whose emotional, feeling, nurturing nature can be directed at the relationship itself. This might produce a tendency to 'mother' your partner, or you might look for maternal qualities in your partner, in order to feel emotionally secure. (An emotionally fulfilling partnership is vitally important to you.)

But the danger with this placement is that you can be overly adaptive to the needs of your partner. In other words, you may find yourself reflecting back to your partner the qualities which you feel he or she needs to complement his or her own. This is the placement of the emotional chameleon.

You share Moon in the Seventh with film star Marilyn Monroe, who died not so much of a drug overdose, as of a lack of self-identity. She tried too hard, and for too long, to be what she thought other people wanted. She mirrored the image of a housewife and baseball fan to Joe Di Maggio; that of a cool intellectual to Arthur Miller, and, at the same time, gave her cinema audiences a dizzy, empty-headed blonde. To every man who desired her, she reflected back the image of a love-goddess. Her Moon sought nurture from her relationships but, in the end, there was nothing to sustain her. No Marilyn. Nothing but a silver reflection.

Mercury in the Seventh needs an intelligent and mentally stimulating partner. You may marry for intellectual companionship and will be drawn to people with whom you can enjoy a meeting of minds. There is also the possibility that you may be strongly attracted to a partner who is your intellectual superior, for Mercury never misses the opportunity to learn something new.

Mercury in the Seventh *has* to communicate. And the person who communicated with an entire generation in the 1960s, with what seemed like a personal message for us all, was Bob Dylan, who shares this placement with you.

A Seventh House Venus needs the closeness and security of a meaningful relationship and seeks a harmonious, romantically fulfilling partnership. To Venus in the Seventh House, marriage 'is the result of the longing for the deep, deep peace of the double bed after the hurly-burly of the chaise longue'.

The Spy Who Loved Me. *Sean Connery put the relating principle of his Seventh House Sun to good effect in portraying James Bond*

Adollf Hitler used his Seventh House sun to impose his will on the masses

With this placement, you are likely to make an ideal partner, for you are considerate and thoughtful and extremely loving. Because you are so accommodating, and motivated to harmonize, and because you want the relationship to be happy, a successful marriage is more than possible. You instinctively know when to give and when to take (although you give far more than you take), and when to compromise for the sake of harmony.

But Venus in the Seventh needs love and consideration lavished on a partner to be returned (and in full measure), and can sometimes be disappointed when this does not materialize. For true happiness, Venus in the Seventh needs to accept that not everyone has such an idealistic view of relating!

Aggressive Mars rushes into the Seventh House, determined to stamp its mark on the relationship. This may lead to a distinctly competitive attitude on Mars's part to be first – to be a 'first among equals', in fact.

There will be a strong sexual basis to the relationship: indeed, this may have been the initial attraction between the parties. Mars in the Seventh cannot be content with a platonic relationship, for the interchange of sexual passion is a necessary part of self-validation.

With this placement, you'll need a partner who is as strong and assertive as you are. You'll have little respect for anyone who is intimidated by your show of strength

and who will, by comparison, make you appear a bully. You – a bully? Who could think such a thing? (Your partner, that's who.)

But, because Mars is short on subtlety at the best of times, and can't dress up its nature in the tissue paper and coloured ribbons of, say, Venus, it's sometimes overlooked that – like the rest of us – you simply want to love and be loved. And you do, don't you? You just have a funny way of showing it, that's all.

Jupiter spreads its benevolent nature over partnerships and love relationships, when found in the Seventh. Unfortunately, this can extend beyond the edges of the relationship and, while you may seek closeness and security with a partner, you may also itch for freedom, and consequently feel restless in your relationships.

Good fortune is likely to accrue as a result of marriage, for it is likely that you will attract — and be attracted to — someone with prospects of material advancement. Jupiter's good judgement is a valuable asset when establishing partnerships!

The nature of your relationships, be they personal or professional, will be honest, warm, generous and open. And the expansionary quality which we have come to associate with Jupiter will lead to a growing awareness of the role played in your life by your 'significant other'.

Where we find Saturn in a chart we find fear and doubt and sometimes pain. It's not surprising, then, that angst-ridden Woody Allen, whose films so often concentrate on his tortuous love-life, should have Saturn sitting firmly on his Descendant!

Saturn in the Seventh takes the whole issue of relationships and partnerships very seriously indeed. The decision to marry may not be taken until later in life, and only after great deliberation. Saturn is frightened of making mistakes, and would rather wait and get it right. Parents of daughters with Saturn in the Seventh need have no fear of midnight elopements!

Saturn represents the principle of limitation and restriction, and so stability, security and clearly established boundaries are sought in a relationship. These qualities may best be found in an older, more mature partner, who is less likely to 'kick over the traces'. Marriage may entail a greater degree of responsibility than usual for Saturn in the Seventh.

With this placement, you'll work hard to make the relationship succeed, and – if there's any justice in this world – your efforts should go a long way to ensure that your marriage is solid, stable and enduring.

Uranus in the Seventh needs freedom to express its unconventional nature. You will be unable to cope with a partner who threatens your independence; you will be drawn to people as independent and individual as you are. Restless, you may find it difficult to sustain what you

see as the dull and inhibiting routine of marriage.

Whereas most people look to a partner to provide the qualities that are missing in themselves, you are attracted to people who seem to require nothing from you. What you *do* need, however, is the acknowledgement of your uniqueness and value as an individual, to calm your fears that your personality may be subsumed in the relationship. Only when you feel free can you join, voluntarily, in partnership with another.

The idealism of Neptune seeks perfection in the Seventh House partner. With this placement, you may

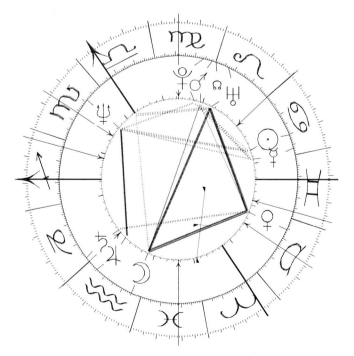

Birth chart (above) of HRH, the Princess of Wales. Partnership, for the former Lady Diana Spencer, allowed her Seventh House Sun to shine as was apparent at her wedding to Prince Charles (right)

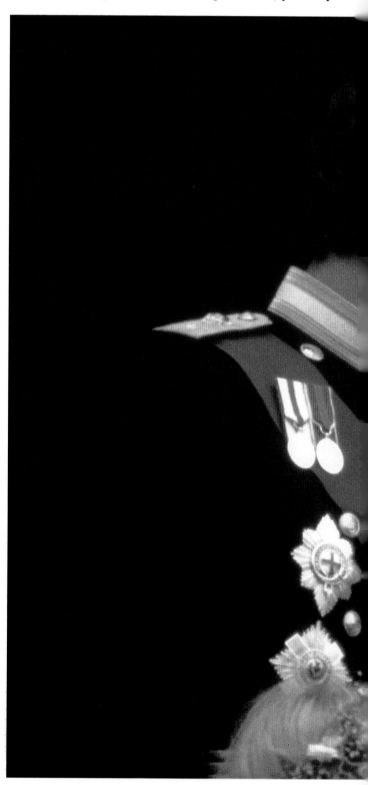

put the beloved on a very high pedestal indeed. Your love is selfless and you seek little in return. It is enough simply to give.

Neptune in the Seventh may manifest itself as a need to 'save' the marriage partner, or possibly to sacrifice one's individuality in order to serve the loved one. Neptune tends to attract lame dogs, and the marital or professional role may be perceived as that of rescuer. Neptune in the Seventh may have a flawed partner – perhaps a heavy drinker or drug abuser – but seeks, through the medium of love, to make the partner whole and perfect again.

With Pluto in the Seventh, you are likely to undergo a personal transformation through marriage or a close relationship. 'Relating' may not be particularly simple for you, since Pluto hauls up complexes from the subconscious, and dumps them firmly in the lap of the partnership. These must be worked through, for the sake of the innocent party: the relationship.

It may be important for you to be the more dominant partner, so that you can control the relationship. But you need to learn that equality can only enhance, and not threaten, a partnership. Only with change, with transformation, can you grow.

THE EIGHTH HOUSE

THE HOUSE OF CHANGE

In some respects, the Eighth House is perhaps the hardest to handle, in terms of life's experiences, in our progress round your Horoscope.

So far, the journey has been relatively easy: establishing your personality and inner resources through the first five Houses, pausing to improve and tidy up in the Sixth, and, in the Seventh, continuing on your way hand-in-hand with a partner.

But the Eighth requires us to call a halt. And (taking a deep breath), to relinquish all that we have so far established, in order that we may take the next step forward – in another direction.

The Eighth is a House of Intimacy, of Shared Resources. Opposite the Second House, which dealt with your personal assets, the Eighth shows you what can be achieved with joint assets; what can be gained by fusing with another.

Let us look into the Second House store cupboards once again. Imagine, this time, that food is in short supply, and is rationed to the staples of life. Your partner has carefully hoarded dried fruits, sugar and flour, whilst you are proud of the secret store of butter, milk and eggs in your cupboard.

Individually, on what will you both dine? On your eggs? On a handful of sultanas? Or will you join forces and combine your ingredients to make a much more nourishing and satisfying cake?

But it's no use contributing your eggs to the potential cake, if you're going to insist they remain whole in their shells so that you may be admired for the generosity of your contribution. Nor can you expect culinary success from eggs that are rolling around a bowl of dry ingredi-

The caterpillar that resists metamorphosis is doomed to die in the cocoon. Change is crucial to survival

ents. So, painful as it may be, you must accept the necessity of their being cracked open so that they can be blended into the mixture, and transformed into a cake.

Ruled by Pluto in the Natural Zodiac, the Eighth House has much to say about the issue of power. It is also traditionally associated with the occult, and the word 'occult' means 'secret', or 'that which is hidden'. And it is the hidden side of our nature that we have to face, and deal with, in this House.

Complexes, compulsions – what used to be called 'hang-ups' – lie festering in the ooze of our subconscious, and occasionally emerge on the surface. They cannot – and should not – be suppressed, but must be resolved through the medium of change. Unless we identify, and transmute, these dark energies, they may engulf and ultimately destroy us.

The old name for the Eighth was 'The House of Death, Sex and Taxes'. For 'Taxes' we can read 'Shared Resources', but 'Death' and 'Sex' are linked together. During our most intimate moments – the sex act – we abandon our sophisticated veneer to reveal our deepest and most hidden thoughts and feelings; to reveal our innermost core. Through sex we may be able to abandon our separateness — and transcend the self — in order to merge with another. Truly satisfying sex demands the 'death' of the ego, in order to achieve mutual ecstasy.

In the Eighth House, therefore, we have to learn to let go of our sense of self – our ego, our separateness – in order to be able to merge. However, to merge doesn't mean simply to share. Merging, in the context of the Eighth House, must involve change. And change is only possible when we accept that one cycle must end, irrevocably, before another can begin, in a new form.

A caterpillar spends several weeks happily munching on leaves, occasionally shedding its skin as it grows into a bigger and stronger caterpillar. But, eventually, it recognizes the fact that it has reached its limits and can grow no more.

If the caterpillar resists change, it will die, for life will be untenable in its present form. But, paradoxically, in order to survive, it must volunteer for death. It must spin a shroud, and willingly relinquish life for the unknown. It has no idea, as its eyes close in sleep, consciousness slips away, and its bodily functions cease, whether Nature will keep faith. It only knows what must be done. It has no idea that, months later, it will emerge into the daylight once again, reborn, metamorphosed, into a beautiful butterfly.

If any man has found his astrologically suitable niche in life, it's *Playboy* Hugh Hefner: not only Mars (his sex-drive) in the Fifth House of Pleasure and Fun, but Sun in the Eighth House of Sex!

Another person with whom you share Sun in the Eighth is President John Kennedy. Jupiter was also in his Eighth House, increasing his aura of power, charisma and sexual magnetism (and sexual appetite, it must be said).

His Eighth House Sun inspired him to rise to the highest position in the country and, in turn, to stimulate his countrymen to change the world for the better. In his inaugural address he said, 'Ask not what America will do for you, but what together we can do for the freedom of man'.

Like President Kennedy, you may be extremely strong-willed, with a powerful personality. You have the strength to overcome your limitations, and rise above disaster. You may find yourself involved with other people's money, through investments, legacies or business finance. Sun in the Eighth also often indicates a strong interest in the occult, or the concept of life after death, and you are very sensitive to psychic undercurrents.

You also share an Eighth House Sun with the despotic King Henry VIII, who irrevocably changed English religion and the role of the monarchy when he severed the ties between the English Church and Rome in 1534. This arose because Henry wished to put away his Queen (who was unable to give him a male heir to ensure the succession) but the Pope refused him the divorce that would enable him to marry his mistress, Anne Boleyn. Eventually the Pope was defied, the monasteries dissolved, the government of the Church reformed, and Henry married a further five times (divorcing two wives and beheading two). All this – basically – for sex! Very Eighth House!

With Sun in the Eighth House, you must rid yourself of all but the very highest of motives, in order to be able

John F. Kennedy: A fairly typical Gemini, but with the forceful willpower of his Eighth House Sun

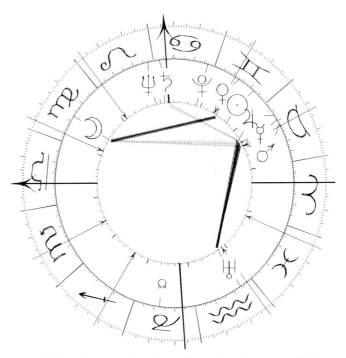

The Eighth House of President Kennedy's chart reveals him as a man of sexual charisma and incredible dynamism

to transcend your limitations.

The feelings and emotions of Moon in the Eighth run very deep indeed. Many difficult or painful issues from the past – maybe even from your very earliest childhood – may rise to the surface again in later life, and your Eighth House task is to learn to purge yourself of them, so that you may move on.

Highly attuned and sensitive responses enable you to tune in to vibrations and undercurrents, and could work strongly in your favour in a business context or when dealing with the public. Sex, for you, is seen as a form of emotional security, comfort and release.

Mercury in the Eighth means secrets! You will either be the ideal confidante, or adept at drawing out other people on personal matters. You'd undoubtedly make a great spy, for Mercury asks questions and wants answers, and Pluto (the natural ruler of this House) makes sure Mercury gets to the bottom of things. However, since the market for spies is strictly limited, a career in forensic detection would be ideal for you. Mercury's focus on detail, allowing you to leave no stone unturned, and Pluto's preoccupation with death, combine brilliantly in the Eighth.

Venus in the Eighth can sometimes indicate financial gains through marriage, or a partnership that is both professional and personal. Venus represents your power to attract money and, in the Eighth, can indicate a financial inheritance or legacy.

Sociable and pleasurable Venus in such a particularly dark House can also indicate romantic jealousy, or per-

'Mad, bad and dangerous to know.' Lord Byron is reputed to have Sun in the Eighth House

Opposite: Change brought about by crisis is a function of the Eighth House. Henry VIII, whose Cancer Sun is reputed to have fallen in the Eighth House of his birth chart, irrevocably changed the face of English religion and the role of the monarchy in 1534 when he severed the ties between the English Church and Rome

haps a more than usually erotic sex life.

Originally (until the discovery of Pluto in 1930) the ruler of this House, Mars brings its assertiveness to the bedroom of the Zodiac. Where Mars is found, will also be found conflict. Tempestuous scenes of great passion are likely, and sex for you is likely to be an exhilarating experience – and a struggle for supremacy!

Mars may have difficulty with the process of merging, thinking it sufficient merely to subdue its aggression, drive for dominance and need to be first at all times. You may have to learn the hard way. You also need to appreciate that your enormous energies and passions – to say nothing of the darker side of your nature – must be controlled and utilized in a more constructive way, if real progress is to be made.

Planets in the Eighth House show our capacity to deal with change brought about by crisis, and Jupiter in the Eighth is convinced that it's an ill wind that blows nobody any good, and that every cloud has a silver lin-

ing. Jupiter sees all of life's experiences in terms of opportunity. Consequently, considering yourself to be a lucky person, and believing that you attract good fortune, you either *do* receive more than your fair share of life's goodies, or else you interpret everything in the best possible terms.

Jupiter in the Eighth can often mean windfalls of 'Other People's Money', as this House was traditionally called. Unexpected tax rebates are not unknown to Jupiter in the Eighth! Unfortunately, however, since Jupiter is the Planet associated with both justice and the law, 'Other People's Money' can frequently involve you in litigation.

You may have an interest in spiritualism, for Jupiter's faith will sustain your belief that there is something else – in another form but definitely better – after death.

Wherever we find Saturn in a chart, we find fear. This is not the easiest of placements to have, for Saturn is under threat in the Eighth House. This Planet is of course motivated to contain, restrict and restrain, and to main-

tain rigid defences. No wonder, then, that Saturn is often alarmed by the thought of intimacy, and by its Eighth House requirement to relinquish control.

Saturn is unused to sharing, and is frightened of losing everything it possesses in the merging process – and that includes Saturn's sense of separateness. This is the most isolated Planet in the Zodiac, and it can't cope too well in the House that calls for the death of the self. Sex can be satisfying physically, but Saturn in the Eighth – crippled by its inability to merge fully – can often experience problems emotionally.

Perhaps the greatest fear for an Eighth House Saturn is what happens when he or she is no longer able to maintain control. The thought of an impotent old age is distressing, and the prospect of corporeal death terrifying. But fear is engendered by ignorance, and with this placement you will find that confronting your fears, and finding out what is likely to happen, will bring spiritual comfort. Elisabeth Kubler-Ross, who has helped so many people make a peaceful transition through the process of dying, shares this placement with you.

Change comes suddenly and unexpectedly to Uranus in the Eighth, and is often triggered by crisis. You may be gifted with insight in such matters as existence on other planes, in other dimensions, thought transference, or telekinesis, and you probably take an intelligent interest in the occult.

The detached and unemotive nature of Uranus is not entirely suited to the deep, dark character of the Eighth, and you may be intrigued by the concept of free love, or tempted by the idea of sexual experimentation.

Since Neptune is characterized by the desire to merge into a state of 'oneness', its needs are more than adequately met in the Eighth House. Sex, with its attendant temporary extinction of the ego – its 'little death', as orgasm was called in Shakespearean times – is an acceptable substitute, as far as Neptune is concerned, for whatever lies beyond consciousness – the state to which Neptune aspires.

Neptune in the Eighth is not entirely problem-free. You may be confused about your sexual identity, or see sex as a form of escapism from reality. Other people's values (shared resources) may turn out to be worthless, or you could be deceived in business. You may be asked to make sacrifices in this most intimate of Houses.

Pluto in the Eighth is in its natural home. With this placement, you will have immense inner strength and internal resources that are hidden from view until precipitated by crisis.

You are phenomenally strong-willed. Life may bring you to your knees, but you will survive, for you have amazing powers of regeneration. You share Pluto in the Eighth House with Bob Geldof, the driving force behind Live Aid. His efforts to generate aid for the famine-stricken populace of Ethiopia, meant new life for countless millions of starving people who had been taken to the brink of death.

Right: Sam Peckinpah – famous for his violent, bloody and overtly sexual films – has Sun in the Eighth House

Opposite: Ludwig van Beethoven, the German composer, is considered to have the Sun in the Eighth

THE
NINTH HOUSE

THE HOUSE OF FAR HORIZONS

After the heavy pressure of the Eighth House and its deep psychological significance, it's good to step into the Ninth House and to have the cobwebs blown away by the winds of enlightenment.

We may have left the Eighth House a little battered, bruised, and bleeding round the edges. We have had to plumb our depths and confront issues which we may have tried to repress or ignore up to the present moment. But we will not have left the Eighth House unchanged. For, if the lessons of the Eighth have been properly learned, we can now consider ourselves a little wiser, a little more evolved, and a little further forward on the path of life.

At this stage of our journey we have emerged, bloodied but unbowed, from the darkness of the Eighth, and now stand on the doorstep of the Ninth, blinking in the unaccustomed sunlight, and trying to see what lies before us. In fact, it's not so much a question of what we can see, as how far we can see, for the Ninth House is the House of the Higher Mind, and its horizons are very far indeed. The Ninth is where we look for our ideals, our truths, faith, philosophy and wisdom. It is where we look for meaning in everything we have learned so far. Whereas the Third House gathers together facts and figures, and snippets of information, the Ninth House teaches us their significance.

On a more mundane level, the Ninth House is associated with different cultures and long-distance travel. Of course, it is entirely possible that you may have sev-

Up, up and away! The House of the Higher Mind (ruled by expansive Jupiter in the Natural Zodiac) allows us to see beyond the mundane. It is also a House of great spirituality, and where we formulate our belief system and ethics

eral Planets in your Ninth House, yet never leave your fireside armchair! But there are no limits to the travels you can make through your mind, for the Ninth is also traditionally associated with higher education.

It is also the place where you find spiritual guidance, principles and your belief system. This is where Jupiter – the Ninth House's ruler in the Natural Zodiac – encourages you to see the big picture, the overall plan. For the Ninth makes you look at life from a different perspective. Somehow, the parameters are higher, wider and further. And, on a clear day, from our Ninth House vantage point, we may even be able to see the purpose of our journey.

From Pluto in the Eighth we go to Sun in the Ninth, where once again we meet Bob Geldof, who masterminded the biggest fund-raising charity event of all time on 13 July 1985. The entire story of *Live Aid* is told in his Ninth House.

Geldof's compassionate Neptune was moved to tears by the suffering of the starving Ethiopians. It was not enough simply to contribute money: sacrificing his own career for nine months, he was driven by Saturn into organizing practical and long-term assistance; into concretizing his vision of 'feeding the world'.

For Geldof, there was no time for patient diplomacy when people were dying. His Mercury/Saturn conjunction went straight for the jugular, cutting through red tape and stripping arguments to the bare bone. He besieged politicians and bureaucrats, bullying them with the force of his Saturn (and charming them with his Libra Sun) until he achieved results. And, with his Ninth House Sun/Saturn/Mercury conjunction aspecting Jupiter in the Third House of Communications, Geldof – for one glorious day – linked the world together.

Bob Geldof mobilized the global conscience. He was

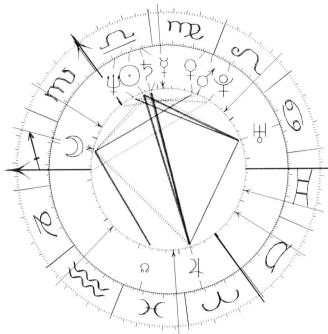

Four Planets – representing compassion, willpower, responsibility and communication – pack the Ninth House of Bob Geldof's chart

responsible not only for organizing the largest rock concert that the world has ever seen, and for raising countless millions for charity, but – even more importantly – for raising our levels of awareness. 'Remember,' he said, 'on the day *you* die, there is someone alive in Africa because one day you watched a pop concert.'

With Sun in the Ninth, you may not be a Geldof, but you can certainly see the big picture in terms of your own life. In fact, you may have your sights set on horizons so far away that you stumble over issues closer to home.

People look for guidance from Sun in the Ninth. You are seen as high-principled, an upholder of the truth. You have a very open approach to life and appreciate the maxim 'The truth shall make you free'; that to know all is to understand all. Mikhail Gorbachev, who introduced the policy of *glasnost* to the Soviet Union, is reputed to have Sun in the Ninth.

You have an optimistic outlook and a very positive personality. You would make a gifted and inspirational teacher. You also share this placement with Rudolf Nureyev, the ballet dancer who defected to the West in his quest for personal freedom, and with Brigitte Bardot, who has abandoned the glamour of her film-star image to rescue ill-treated and abandoned animals.

With Moon in the Ninth, you may have spent your early years outside your native country, or may be an inveterate traveller during your adult life, for you are extremely restless and constantly on the move. You may make emotional relationships with people from a different country or culture. Your quest may be of a culinary nature, for Moon in the Ninth (like Moon in Sagittarius)

Feed the world. Geldof's personal moment of triumph. 13 July 1985, Wembley Stadium

often means a love of foreign food!

Philosophies and principles are likely to have been adopted, unconsciously, from your parents, and you may regard your mother as the guiding force in your life. You share this placement with American actor Robert De Niro.

Mercury in the Ninth seeks a wider understanding of all the knowledge it has gleaned along the way. You may be interested in the workings of the law, or you may be involved in higher education. You have a curious mind,

a lively intelligence, and probably an extensive library of books that will enrich your intellectual store. You are keen to pass on what you have learned to others.

Venus in the Ninth is, on the whole, a pleasant and comfortable placement. You enjoy life in general. You may have a love of travel and foreign cultures, and probably mix easily with people of all races and countries. You could be romantically attracted to someone from a foreign country – a holiday romance is always a possibility with Venus in the Ninth!

Nostradamus, the sixteenth-century French astrologer, whose coded predictions have proved uncannily accurate, had Sun in the Ninth

MICHEL NOSTRADAMUS.
Médecin,
Né à St Remy, en Provence, le 14 Décemb. 1503.
Mort le 2 juillet 1566.

You have a developed sense of aesthetic appreciation, and enjoy browsing in art galleries and visiting churches and other old buildings. Great peace of mind is derived from your religious or spiritual values.

Aggressively idealistic with Mars in the Ninth, you'll fight for your values and principles, for this is the placement of the crusader. You're the first to try anything new or adventurous, if you think it will broaden your experience or outlook, and you pursue your goals with great energy.

Mars in the Ninth is commonly found in the birth charts of champion sportsmen and athletes, and you are likely to have a keen interest in competitive sports. You share Mars in the Ninth with Mohammed Ali, the boxer.

The Ninth House is home to Jupiter in the Natural Zodiac, and it's the place where Jupiter is at its most expansive. A high moral code and a philosophical outlook usually accompany Jupiter in the Ninth. You look

for meaning in everything you experience, and generally try to see the positive side of life.

Religion, for you, is not simply the source of spiritual comfort, but a means of expanding your understanding of the Cosmos. Religious studies may be pursued, partly as a means of learning about other cultures.

The importance of broadening your outlook and acquiring knowledge cannot be over-estimated, and your aim in life is to share your knowledge with others. You would make an excellent teacher in higher education. Fair-minded and tolerant, your sense of justice could also indicate an interest in the law. The Ninth House is where we abandon the superficial elements of our lives for a broader and more humanitarian approach.

You share this placement with Robert Redford, whose life as a screen star now takes second billing to

Sun in the Ninth Brigitte Bardot, who has abandoned the glamour and superficiality of her film-star lifestyle for the important things in life

his work teaching others at his Sundance Institute.

There is little spirit of adventure with Saturn in the Ninth. Rigid thought formations are uncomfortable in the House of mind expansion; Saturn cannot reach very far with folded arms. The secret of success with this placement is to work with Saturn's nature, rather than trying to fight it. Let Saturn develop in its own slow, deliberate way. You are concerned to be seen, and respected, as a strongly moral character who is totally above reproach. There is a conservative outlook on learning and, with Saturn in the Ninth, hard work leads to academic achievement. Traditional methods of higher education – universities, colleges – are favoured, rather than seeking enlightenment from a guru.

You find it hard to grasp loose concepts of the meaning of life, and require sensible answers to your questions. You give much careful thought to what may be your purpose in life, and prefer to structure its growth and development so that progress is under control.

Saturn is the last Planet to go hitch-hiking round the world, whistling merrily on its way. You are not one of life's 'back-packers'. Long-distance travel, for you, is likely to be undertaken mainly for business purposes, or for the educational benefits it can bring, rather than for sheer pleasure.

The Ninth House is concerned with truth, justice and meaning, and Uranus in this House seeks enlightenment in unorthodox ways. Conventional religion, for

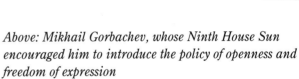

Above: Mikhail Gorbachev, whose Ninth House Sun encouraged him to introduce the policy of openness and freedom of expression

Left: Rudolf Nureyev, who made a gigantic leap for freedom when he asked for and was granted political asylum while performing in Paris in 1961, has Sun in the Ninth House

instance, may be cursorily examined and then discarded in favour of the theory of reincarnation. Tried and tested educational methods may be abandoned for 'hothouse' practices. Bizarre cults could hold out the promise of Utopia.

With this placement you are likely to keep an open mind, and to be receptive to new ideas and unusual concepts. Travel is likely to be undertaken on the spur of the moment and may provide experiences which will give you fresh insight and clearer understanding.

Neptune in this House looks for spiritual enlightenment through mystic channels. There may be a strong interest in transcendental meditation or yoga but, with this placement, you should be aware that impressionable Neptune is vulnerable to deception by idealistic cults that promise Nirvana. A badly aspected Neptune in the Ninth may look for chemical means of mind expansion; drink and drugs are the dangers here. Travel, for you, is physical escapism; higher education is a means of escaping the limitations of the mind.

With Pluto in the Ninth, you'll be driven to look further, and deeper, for the meaning of life. Crisis may have prompted you to change, or formulate, your life philosophies and moral standards. Your thinking is profound, and you are not afraid to discard the values and beliefs you once held dear, and all that has gone before, and to replace it with shining truth. This placement often confers qualities of leadership.

THE
TENTH HOUSE

THE HOUSE OF PRESTIGE AND AUTHORITY

The late Noël Coward was famous for the song which began, 'Mad dogs and Englishmen go out in the midday sun' – the Sun is of course at its most visible and most powerful when it culminates (reaches its highest position overhead) at noon. Culmination is represented on your birth chart by the MC (*Medium Coeli*, or Midheaven), which forms the cusp of your Tenth House, the last of the Angular Houses.

As we have seen, the opposite end of this axis (the IC) forms the cusp of the Fourth House, which is concerned with the hidden, unconscious side of the personality. By contrast, the Tenth House is very much part of the public domain, and Tenth House activities are played out under the spotlight, to a fanfare of trumpets.

The 'spotlight' is the very essence of the Tenth House, for this is where we enjoy our 'fifteen minutes of fame' and are at our most visible. It is where we make public our ambitions, and show how those ambitions manifest themselves. The Tenth House, then, can be a useful pointer to an ideal career.

Personality and character can be considered four-sided. The Ascendant shows the initial impression you make; the Moon shows your instinctive, unconscious nature; and the Sun Sign shows your will and purpose. But the MC shows your self-view; shows the image and the qualities which you would like other people to see.

The Tenth House is where we want to receive acknowledgement and credit for what we are, as well as what we have achieved; where we seek applause and respect, and validation of our status. In such a sensitive

How we make our mark on society, and what we would like to be remembered for, is indicated by the Tenth House. It is concerned with status, and the culmination of our ambition

House, therefore, planets play an especially important role in indicating what we would like to be credited, applauded and respected for.

Sun in the Tenth has a burning desire to be special. There is a great need to be acknowledged as successful, powerful and important. With this placement, driving ambition and the will to succeed are usually masked by a dignified and controlled exterior, for Sun in the Tenth House has to have authority, 'presence' and prestige.

You share this high-profile placement with three statesmen: France's Jacques Delors, Russia's Nikita Khruschev, and US President George Bush. Napoleon Bonaparte, who rose from humble artillery officer to become Emperor of the French, holding all Europe under his sway, is also reputed to have had a Tenth House Sun.

A career which can enhance your public position and social standing is important to you. If it is not possible for you to develop a career of your own, then it is likely that you will be drawn to a successful partner who can provide you with prestige and status by proxy.

A career that confers status, and approbation from the public, is what you seek with Moon in the Tenth. This could be achieved with relative ease, for you will have an instinctive understanding of what the public wants.

You may come from a family of 'high-flyers', or your mother may have instilled ambition in you. (She is likely to have been an achiever, and perhaps the driving force of the family.)

Communicative skills, an agile brain and bright ideas accompany Mercury in the Tenth. With this placement, you will have a fine appreciation of the role that education can play in the furtherance of career issues. You will

want to be appreciated as an educated and clever person, and will use your knowledge in the pursuance of career opportunities.

You share Mercury in the Tenth House with Marconi, inventor of the wireless telegraph system.

Venus in the Tenth wants to be loved and appreciated simply for being Venus. Social ambition usually accompanies this placement. You want to be seen as attractive and stylish, and you are attracted to people with good connections who can enhance your status and advance your social progress. Your professional role will invariably utilize your gifts of tact and diplomacy, and your sense of good taste.

You share Mars in the Tenth House with Vincent van Gogh. With energetic Mars conjoined to artistic Venus in the Tenth, van Gogh painted furiously for the last four years of his life, desperate to achieve fame, but remaining totally unappreciated. The stressful aspect from his emotional Moon in the Fifth House of Creativity to the Venus/Mars conjunction in the Tenth House of Prestige, tells us of the artistic frustration and lack of recognition which led to van Gogh's self-mutilation and eventual suicide.

Mars in the Tenth may not drive you to the extent of slicing off your ear, like van Gogh, but it will fuel you with a burning ambition to succeed, and give you the strength and determination to fight your way to the top.

You are extremely competitive in business, and will not content yourself with anything less than a high managerial or executive position. Since Saturn is the ruler of this House in the Natural Zodiac, your Martian energy is tempered by Saturn's control and structured approach to your life-goals.

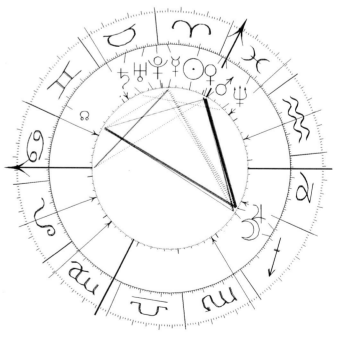

Anger and furious energy are shown by the placement of Mars in the Tenth House of Vincent van Gogh's birth chart

*Right: Never was there a
more ambitious man than
Napoleon Bonaparte,
whose reputed Ten House
Sun drove him to create
an empire that stretched
across the whole of Europe*

*Opposite: George Bush,
a man of quiet
dignified authority*

Jupiter in the Tenth House wishes to be seen as a dignified and respected member of the community, and a benefactor of society. With this placement you will project an image of wisdom and fair-mindedness, and public recognition of these qualities will bolster your self-validation. You seek fame.

Saturn works well in the Tenth House (its natural home), for it confers self-discipline, cold calculating ambition, and an iron will to succeed. But 'flash-in-the-pan' fame is not your idea of success. You crave solid respectability, status, public recognition of your qualities and appreciation of your traditional, conservative values. Most of all, you want authority. And you are well aware that success of this kind is acquired only through unremitting hard work and determination.

Uranus in the Tenth wants to be appreciated for being 'different'. This placement may involve you in many changes of career, for your innovative and original approach rarely accords with the traditional amd conservative values of the Establishment.

Karl Marx, who founded the political and economic system of modern Socialism, shares Uranus in the Tenth with you.

There are several ways in which a Tenth House Neptune may manifest its nature. It may cloud the whole issue of the ideal career, leaving you confused about the best direction to take. In any event, Neptune in the Tenth ensures that yours will be no ordinary career. Neptune's refining qualities may inspire you to the greatest heights. It may bestow artistic or musical tal-

Left: Nikita Khrushev, the former Soviet premier, had Sun (in Aries) in the Tenth House. A true Aries, he combined a volatile nature with naive simplicity, and the Tenth House placement of his Sun gave iron strength to his determination, and force to his arguments

Opposite: Jack Nicolson – famous for being Jack Nicolson! This immensely popular actor has certainly reached the top of the bill in his profession.

ent, or the gifts of mysticism and clairvoyance.

Neptune may also require a sacrifice as the price of fame. Or it may set you on a pedestal and represent you in a very idealistic light indeed, for Neptune in the Tenth is the 'fairy princess and film star' placement. It is no coincidence, therefore, that Diana, Princess of Wales, shares this placement with you.

Pluto brings its unbreakable will to your career when found in the Tenth House. You will experience an overwhelming desire to succeed, and will allow nothing to stand in your way.

Former President Richard Nixon, who shares this placement with you, wanted power at all costs, and his desire for omnipotence eventually brought about his downfall through the Watergate scandal. Pluto in the Tenth, therefore, has to learn to use its power for the improvement of society as a whole, and not self-aggrandisement.

THE TENTH HOUSE AND CAREER

The Tenth House is where we look for specific pointers to the ideal career. Since each Sign of the Zodiac can be assigned to various occupational and vocational paths,

check the Sign on the cusp (the beginning) of your Tenth House, and compare it with the table below.

If you do not know your time of birth, you will be unable to ascertain your Ascendant nor, by extension, will you be able to determine the Sign on your Tenth House cusp. In that event, ask your local astrologer to prepare a Solar chart for you. This will assume your Ascendant to be at the same degree of the Zodiac as your Sun, and the Houses will be numbered accordingly.

Therefore, with a Solar chart, if your 'Ascendant' is in the Sign of:

ARIES your 'Tenth House' will be in CAPRICORN
TAURUS your 'Tenth House' will be in AQUARIUS
GEMINI your 'Tenth House' will be in PISCES
CANCER your 'Tenth House' will be in ARIES
LEO your 'Tenth House' will be in TAURUS
VIRGO your 'Tenth House' will be in GEMINI
LIBRA your 'Tenth House' will be in CANCER
SCORPIO your 'Tenth House' will be in LEO
SAGITTARIUS your 'Tenth House' will be in VIRGO
CAPRICORN your 'Tenth House' will be in LIBRA
AQUARIUS your 'Tenth House' will be in SCORPIO
PISCES your 'Tenth House' will be in SAGITTARIUS

Martin Luther King. A Tenth House Sun gave this much-loved and well-respected man a very high profile

THE TENTH HOUSE CUSP IN ARIES
- Soldier
- Explorer
- Surgeon
- Metallurgist
- Butcher
- Cutler
- Blacksmith
- Dentist

THE TENTH HOUSE CUSP IN TAURUS
- Model
- Farmer
- Financier
- Art dealer
- Singer
- Property dealer
- Cook
- Florist

THE TENTH HOUSE CUSP IN GEMINI
- Teacher
- Journalist
- Secretary
- Writer
- Linguist

THE TENTH HOUSE CUSP IN CANCER
- Sailor
- Hotelier
- Caterer
- Midwife
- Governess

THE TENTH HOUSE CUSP IN LEO
- Chairman
- Jeweller
- Goldsmith
- Party planner

THE TENTH HOUSE CUSP IN VIRGO
- Secretary
- Statistician
- Accountant
- Critic
- Health worker
- Craftsman
- Doctor

THE TENTH HOUSE CUSP IN LIBRA
- Diplomat
- Artist
- Model
- Beautician

THE TENTH HOUSE CUSP IN SCORPIO
- Forensic scientist
- Surgeon
- Coroner
- Undertaker
- Psychoanalyst
- Detective
- Pharmacist
- Plumber
- Waste disposal worker

THE TENTH HOUSE CUSP IN SAGITTARIUS
- Publisher
- Lawyer
- Jockey
- Travel agent
- Minister of religion
- Philosopher
- Sportsman

THE TENTH HOUSE CUSP IN CAPRICORN
- Osteopath
- Politician
- Civil servant
- Antiques dealer
- Builder
- Architect

THE TENTH HOUSE CUSP IN AQUARIUS
- Scientist
- Astrologer
- Inventor
- Radiologist
- Television broadcaster
- Ecologist.

THE TENTH HOUSE CUSP IN PISCES
- Anaesthetist
- Medium/Clairvoyant
- Oil worker
- Poet
- Musician
- Actor
- Deep-sea fisherman

THE
ELEVENTH HOUSE

The realization that no further progress can be made as an individual comes at the Eleventh House. Our journey round the birth chart has enabled us to identify ten different stages of development, from the first inkling of our individuality to the establishment of status. And, if we return to the original analogy of an architect's blueprint, we could liken this progress to the construction of a marvellous office block, ten storeys high, beautifully furnished and fully equipped, and admired as a masterpiece of design and execution.

But an empty building is a waste. To justify the time, cost and effort involved in its erection, it must play its part in the life of the city. And, by the same token, the individual must play his or her part within the overall system.

Let us look again at the genesis of Live Aid. It began with a note, stuck on Bob Geldof's refrigerator door, that said: 'Everyone who visits this house from today onwards will be asked to give £5 until we have raised £200 for famine relief.'

The escalation of the target figure of £200 to the £87,000,000 raised nine months later is history. And it was achieved through the simple principle of the Eleventh House: each person involved with Live Aid contributed his individual talent to the common pool, and individual egos were extinguished in favour of the common good.

The Eleventh House, then, shows what we may achieve by tailoring our personal goals to the needs of

Sometimes, co-operation achieves far more than personal effort. The Eleventh House shows the creative expression of a group working in harmony

society, and teaches us that the endeavours of a co-ordinated group can achieve more than the sum of several individual efforts. Opposite the Fifth House of personal creativity, the Eleventh shows the creative expression of an organization working in harmony: one slave alone cannot move a block of stone, but thousands working in unison built the Pyramids.

Whereas Fifth House creativity is linked to the sex drive and personal pleasure, the nature of the Eleventh House, however, is totally asexual and impersonal. There is no self-gratification to be had from the Eleventh House. It is a House of cerebral and spiritual universality.

We have learned, through our astrological journey, that it is not possible for an individual to exist in a vacuum; in isolation. We have to make our responses to society. Even a recluse like Howard Hughes required a support system in order to sustain his seclusion. And it is in the Eleventh House that we can see how we integrate into the group; how we operate within the larger system.

The traditional name for the Eleventh House was the House of Hopes, Dreams and Wishes. It has been described as the Realm of Communal Spirit; the House of Friends; the House of Idealism. Planets in this House may indicate the type of friends who attract us, common interests, and how we pursue our goals.

This is the dawning of the Age of Aquarius, we are told, and the eleventh Sign of the Zodiac is, of course, Aquarius. Every day, in little ways, we are slowly moving towards the Aquarian dream of Utopia. We are beginning to develop global awareness, and to take global responsibility for our planet. Through the ecology movement, we are beginning the task of saving our planet for future generations. Through the United Nations, we are working towards global jurisdiction and political co-operation. Day by day, we are beginning to understand that we are globally interdependent, and that the concept of 'I'm all right, Jack' has no place in the Eleventh House.

In the Age of Aquarius we are learning to fight for worldwide justice, freedom, democracy and humanitarian ideals. We are becoming aware of the need to aid the world's under-privileged, and to feed the world's hungry. And at last, through our Eleventh House consciousness, we are beginning to realize exactly what our tiny, individual contributions, multiplied worldwide, can mean.

Sun in the Eleventh House spells 'campaigner', for you share this placement with America's black presidential candidate Jesse Jackson; political activist and actress Jane Fonda; evangelist Billy Graham; and former UK prime minister Margaret Thatcher.

Margaret Thatcher fought throughout her political career for her passionately held ideals of freedom: freedom of choice; freedom from the stranglehold of the unions; freedom from international terrorism; freedom for economic development. She is held in high esteem worldwide for the driving force of her Eleventh House ideals.

An Eleventh House Sun confers group leadership and, as we have seen, is the mark of the freedom fighter. You tend to identify totally with the aims of your peers, and you will have many friends – some with influence and leadership qualities themselves – who will admire you for your strength of character and radical thinking.

The nurturing side of the Moon may mean that you take a maternal attitude to group activities, hosting coffee mornings for discussion groups, organizing PTA meetings, or running the local Scout pack.

Moon in the Eleventh House finds security in numbers. You may have few really close friends, but many acquaintances with whom you share interests in common.

Mercury in the Eleventh likes to learn in company. You welcome the exchange of ideas and viewpoints, and are always willing to add to your store of knowledge from such encounters.

This is a good placement for Mercury. It bestows impartial thinking and clear objectivity, and a degree of foresightedness. There is a love of debate. Often, Mercury in the Eleventh becomes the spokesman of the group. Winston Churchill advised America in 1954 that 'to jaw-jaw is better than to war-war', and Mercury in the Eleventh feels there are no problems – even critical world situations – which cannot be solved by negotiation and discussion.

Venus brings its reconciliatory powers to the Eleventh, promoting harmony and co-operation in group endeavours. You are motivated to use your civilizing influence for the benefit of the group.

You will have many like-minded friends, who may seek to improve society in some way. You are keen to cultivate friends who may advance you socially, and you are likely to marry someone from your own social circle.

Mars can sometimes be a little too self-centred to fit comfortably into the Eleventh House of Idealism, and needs to learn how to turn its assertiveness to the benefit of others – how to fight for the group's interests, in other words.

Left: Eleventh House Sun Jesse Jackson – a political campaigner of great stature

Opposite: 'The Realm of Communal Spirit'. Eleventh House Sun Bob Hope entertains the troops with his Geminian wit as his contribution to the group endeavour

With Mars in the Eleventh you will have many friends who are just as assertive as you, or who will spur you to action. You are capable of using your enormous energies for the common good, and can be an effective organizer. You are likely to have stimulating, passionate (and sometimes quarrelsome) relationships with your friends.

Jupiter in theEleventh is the placement of the humanitarian. Jupiter wants to benefit everybody, on the largest possible scale. Its expansive and generous nature inspires group endeavour to strive for 'the greatest good for the greatest number'.

With Jupiter in the Eleventh House of your Horoscope, you will receive moral and spiritual sustenance from your many warm-spirited friends who, in turn, will look to you for benevolent support. You will be drawn to organizations that foster the spirit of egalitarianism and the welfare of the less fortunate.

Saturn is not noted for its qualities as a social mixer, and sometimes fares badly in the Eleventh House. However, there is none the less a great sense of responsibility towards others and, in a group situation, this may take the form of organizational commitments, obligation and a patriarchal attitude towards the group members.

With Saturn in this House, you may find it hard to drop your defences sufficiently to form friends and integrate with a group but, once you have overcome this barrier, such relationships you do make are likely to be enduring and sincere.

Uranus is on home ground in the Eleventh House. You are open-minded and a true free thinker. Extremely idealistic in an impartial, detached way, you have a clear, unbiased view of society as a whole, although your remedies for righting the world's ills may appear radical and drastic to others who are less enlightened.

You mix well in groups. Humanitarian and ecological issues claim your attention, and you could be interested in groups involved in scientific or occult studies, electronics or cybernetics.

Your idealism extends to your friendships. You expect friends to be as open with you as you are with them, and to share your goals.

Uranus in the Eleventh has a fresh perspective, an unusual viewpoint, of the world. One person who shares this placement with you, Buzz Aldrin, the astronaut, certainly saw the world from an unusual viewpoint – the Moon!

Compassionate Neptune weeps for the world's pain

Margaret Thatcher: Unmindful of her personal popularity, her Eleventh House Sun spurred her to campaign for what she perceived as the common good, and her passionately-held ideals of freedom

Evangelist Billy Graham is driven by his Eleventh House Sun to 'spread the word'. His Sun is in Scorpio – the Sign most closely associated with 'rebirth'

when found in the Eleventh House. You are likely to be an extremely altruistic person, with the idealistic goal of a truly Utopian society. You would readily sacrifice your personal wishes if you thought you could benefit society in any way by your action.

You are the champion of the underdog. You are kind and generous to your friends, and sensitive to their needs. In return, they are equally generous in extending support and guidance to you.

If badly aspected in this House, Neptune may be susceptible to seduction or diversion from the original goals of the group, or may be in danger of deception as to the group's aims and ideals. And, of course, Neptune's escapist tendencies might blur the group's objectives by holding group meetings in the local wine bar or pub!

Pluto in the Eleventh House indicates a social or political reformer; one who brings about change through crisis, through tearing down the old order and generating the new.

As a friend, your loyalty is deep and enduring (there is nothing superficial about Pluto). But jealousy or power struggles may arise, and any severance of the friendship is likely to be bitter, and irrevocable.

With this placement, you can occupy a position of great power within the group, and can use your strength to motivate the group to change society for the better.

Opposite: Eleventh House Sun Jane Fonda, idealistic political campaigner, also united millions of women in 'going for the burn'

144

THE
TWELFTH HOUSE

THE HOUSE OF BURIED TREASURE

'The House of Buried Treasure' is not the best-known name for this House, which has been given many labels: The Realm of Concealment; The House of Secret Enemies; The House of Karma. And, perhaps the most poetic of all: The House of Self-Undoing and Sustainment. Perhaps this last name explains best the nature of the last of the twelve Houses on our journey through your Horoscope. For the Twelfth House shows us that our worst 'secret enemy' is the one within us; that we are the authors of our own misfortune. Conversely, and at the same time, we are our own greatest source of strength, our sustainment.

The Twelfth House corresponds to the twelfth Sign, Pisces, and is ruled in the Natural Zodiac by Neptune.

Neptune's function is to remove barriers – not by tearing them down, like Pluto, but by dissolving them. Neptune would like everything rendered to a state of liquid suspension; to be formless; to be returned to the state of primeval nebulousness that existed in the Beginning. And the Twelfth House represents our acknowledgement of that 'pre-existence', and our acceptance that, since life is cyclical, we must rejoin it at the end of our cycle; that we must go back to where we started. Like E.T., we must 'go home'.

It is at the point of the Twelfth House that we acknowledge we are not the be-all and end-all of Creation, that there is something far greater than we can possibly comprehend.

It is commonly assumed that astrology and religion (particularly Christian religion) are mutually incompatible. This need not be so. Whether you believe in the promise of life after death, reincarnation, or the concept of *karma*, you are nevertheless accepting that the Universe is a continually evolving cycle of formation, dissolution and re-formation.

If you are a relative beginner in astrology, the concept of *karma* may be new to you. Basically, *karma* is a Buddhist term (of Sanskrit origin) for the law of cause and effect as expressed by Sir Isaac Newton's postulate: 'For every action there is an equal and opposite reaction.' Or, as the Bible phrases it, 'As ye sow, so shall ye reap'.

The karmic principle of astrology is that the soul selects a time to be born when the planetary pattern for that moment indicates an appropriate Horoscope ('earned' by the previous incarnation) for the current incarnation. Planets in the Twelfth House, therefore, show what you are carrying in your astrological suitcase to assist or hinder you on the present journey.

We need to think of *karma* as a cosmic savings account; where we earn credit for our next incarnation through the actions of this one. A belief in *karma* promulgates the idea of 'jam tomorrow'. We should not look, therefore, for immediate rewards from the Twelfth House. It is a House where we act selflessly, with no thought of reciprocal benefit: a House where we give, and do not count the cost.

The Twelfth is also known as the repository for the collective unconscious – a cosmic 'soup' of memory, thought and experience – and the storehouse for universal potential. We can look into the Twelfth and see not only what contributed to our past, but what is lying dormant for our future.

The Twelfth House is also known as the House of Retreat and Institutions. On a mundane level, the Twelfth is associated with hospitals, asylums, religious

When we reach the Twelfth House, there's nowhere else to go but home; the cycle is complete. But what lies beyond?

147

retreats, prisons – anywhere, in fact, where the individual can find solitude .

Hopefully, we will experience neither prison nor psychiatric hospitalization during our lifetime. But we all need periods of isolation, and we all need places to which we can retreat, in order to lick our wounds and find our inner strength. The Twelfth House has much to say about the way in which we escape from the pressures of our daily life, and Planets in the Twelfth House describe our inner strengths – the 'buried treasure' – we can draw on.

When we reach the Twelfth House, there's nowhere else to go but home, and nothing else to do but dissolve our separate, unique identity in order to unite with something infinitely greater.

Let us return to our original analogy for a moment. We can say that our astrological journey has been similar to tracing the progress of a building from blueprint to foundation stone to 'topping out' There is nothing further which can be added. The building is complete. And yet, in the Twelfth, we are asked to demolish the building, to destructure what we have established, and to reduce it to its component parts: bricks, mortar, joists, roof tiles, windows and doors.

We should be happy to do so. For if we all pool our bricks, our joists and tiles, our windows and doors, we should be able to raise an edifice that will stretch into infinity.

Sun in the Twelfth is a polarization of planetary principles, for the Sun represents personal will and conscious actions, while the Twelfth House represents the opposite. One of the effects of Sun in the Twelfth House, therefore, is that watery Neptune may negate your individuality, and you may suffer a lack of strong self-identity. Of course, the positive side of this is that Neptune infiltrates its compassionate, sensitive nature into your personality, enhancing your receptiveness and empathy.

Sun in the Twelfth works best (and most often) behind the scenes. You can be described as the power behind the throne. Your face and name may not be known to many, but the work that you do is.

In order to achieve fulfilment, you will have to find some way of incorporating Neptune's sacrifical nature into your life: hospital or prison visiting would enable you to serve others, and help discharge the liability of karmic debt which Sun in the Twelfth often represents.

You share this placement with Henry Kissinger. Mahatma Gandhi is reputed to have had Sun in the Twelfth House, too.

Sun in the Twelfth can manifest itself in more than one way. Henry Kissinger (opposite), the diplomat, characterises the 'power behind the throne' aspect, while Mahatma Gandhi (below) displaying this House's Neptunian side, was prepared to sacrifice his life for his political and religious ideas

The Moon in this sector of your chart can indicate a nature well attuned to Twelfth House principles. Because the Moon is associated with instinctive reactions and attitudes from our earliest childhood, you may be able to make easy psychic and intuitive links with your subconscious and the collective unconscious. None the less, you may reluctant to be open about your emotions, preferring to keep them hidden.

Your Moon is only too willing to dissolve into the infinite, so that you may be at one with the Cosmos. You are immensely compassionate and imaginative.

You share this placement with George Harrison.

With Mercury in the Twelfth House of Self-Undoing, muddled or negative thinking could result from Neptune's foggy influence. But let us not forget that the House of Self-Undoing is also the House of Sustainment! With this placement, you may have to learn to let go of rationale in favour of developing the 'buried treasure' of your imagination.

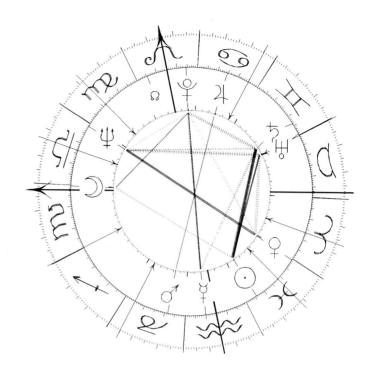

The birth chart of George Harrison. A former Beatle, adored and adulated worldwide, he has lived simply and quietly since the seventies. His chart shows the Moon placed in the Twelfth House, indicating that solitude and a place of retreat are of great importance to him. For many years he sought spiritual guidance from mystics and gurus, and he is sustained by his evolved spiritual awareness.
The Moon rules the emotions and, in the Twelfth House, is coloured by the compassionate nature of Neptune – the ruler of this House in the Natural Zodiac. George Harrison's heart was touched by the sorry plight of the Kampucheans, and his concert for Kampuchea was the forerunner of the wave of charity concerts staged in subsequent years.

Opposite: Laurence Oliver, who escaped into fantasy through his theatrical roles

Venus in the Twelfth is sometimes asked to make sacrifices in the name of love. In this placement, Venus wants love to be perfect, without limitation or boundary, and perhaps the sacrifice that Venus must make is the expectation of reciprocation. Venus's love may have to stay hidden, and unsung.

You are likely to be very artistic, or musical, and inspired by the wealth of your unconscious mind.

Mars may have problems in the House of Secret Enemies. For what is hidden away, and what becomes Mars's 'enemy' is anger, uncontained and directionless in the Twelfth House. You should identify what could manifest itself as futile anger, and learn to convert it into energy which can be used for the common good.

Jupiter in the Twelfth bestows an unconscious confidence that 'It'll be all right on the night' – that nothing can go seriously wrong in life. You regard this Planet as a sort of astrological guardian angel.

This sublime optimism is carried all through life. Because you believe yourself to be fortunate, you attract good fortune (or the opportunities that can lead to it). And the presence of beneficial Jupiter in your karmic suitcase for this incarnation is nothing more than a fitting reward for your behaviour in the last.

You may spend time alone, in introspective study of the meaning of your life's journey, and you will eventually discover that all your riches come from within.

Whereas Saturn was merely frightened at the prospect of losing control during the merging process of the Eighth House, Saturn is *terrified* of losing its individuality – its identity – by the process of dissolving into the Twelfth. Working for the benefit of others (particularly those in institutions) may do much to convince you that the barriers preventing you from lessening your fears through confrontation, are entirely self-imposed.

Uranus in the Twelfth is not afraid to make conceptual leaps in the dark towards enlightenment. Uranus knows that there is more to life than is readily apparent, and appreciates that this can be reached by tapping into a higher mental plane. You have a highly developed sense

'Escapism' expressed through a Twelfth House Sun: Judy Garland, who tragically sought escape through drink and drugs

Opposite: 'Miss Saigon' – a story of Neptunian love, and Twelfth House sacrifice

of intuition, and may display uncanny foresight or a degree of clairvoyance.

Neptune in the Twelfth – in its natural home, in fact – urges you to 'tune in, turn on, drop out'. The tuning-in can have very positive results, for your sensitive appreciation of planetary vibrations can be used for artistic creativity, spiritual sustainment and psychic healing. Turning-on and dropping-out, however, are manifestations of Neptune at its most negative – an escape route through the medium of alcohol or drugs to an artificial Nirvana.

President Bush shares this placement with you, and his Twelfth House tells an apt story of his service in World War Two. With Mars (the aggressive Planet of War) fighting dutifully from the Sixth House, but prepared to die for Twelfth House ideals, President Bush's aeroplane was shot down by enemy fire into the Neptunian Pacific!

With Pluto in the Twelfth House of spiritual unity, you have perhaps the greatest astrological gift of all – if you are not afraid to use it. It is the gift of power. The power to render evil into good; to grow through pain into peace.

Pluto's energy is dark, and can be overwhelming in its potency. But, with courage, its ruthless strength can be used to purge and regenerate and, in the Twelfth House, to transcend its limitations to merge into perfect Oneness.

THE
FINAL WORD

I t is not the purpose of this book to attempt a compre-
hensive analysis of your birth chart, but to open your
eyes to what a chart can tell you, to act as a guide, and
to whet your appetite to find out more. Above all, the aim
is to make you aware of the richness, depth and breadth
of your personality.

A Horoscope can only indicate predispositions,
potential, what *may* come to pass and not what undoubtedly *will*. For what no book can show you is the effect of
our greatest personal asset: free will.

The exercise of free will is what makes us unique as
a species. We can choose to fight adversity, or we can
choose to succumb to it. We are not planetary 'victims'
at the mercy of the Zodiac. Astrology can show us what
choices are likely to be open to us, but the final decision
is ours and ours alone. Your Horoscope may pinpoint a
musical talent, for instance, but free will motivates you
to learn an instrument, and then to practise. Or not, as
the case may be.

The interpretations given in this book are not to be
applied rigidly or literally, but adapted to your personal
situation and circumstances.

Because you may be unmarried and live alone, for
instance, there is certainly no need to ignore the chap-
ter on the Seventh House of Relationships. Read it in the
light of your circumstances. References to sporting
competitiveness may seem irrelevant if, say, you are
physically disabled. But perhaps you're a Trivial Pursuit
champion, or a madly competitive Bridge player? Interpret the planetary pattern of your chart in the light of
what is relevant, and disregard what is not.

Astrology is often criticised for appearing equivocal.
For instance, as a broad analogy, it could be said that a
mass murderer, who hacks his victims to death, and a
surgeon, who uses the knife to save life and reduce suffering, may both have an interest in the human body and
surgery! Individual interpretation will vary of course,
according to circumstances and viewpoint: a strongly
Saturnian nature will describe a glass as half-empty,
while Jupiter will describe it as half-full.

At the very beginning of this book, we likened a
Horoscope to a road map. We said it could warn you of
hazards, suggest shortcuts, show you alternative
routes. Hopefully, it will show you the way to a more fulfilling appreciation of your talents and characteristics,
and help make your journey through Life more interesting and rewarding.

It is a *map*, and not the destination itself. And you
cannot blame the cartographer if you persist in reading
it upside down.

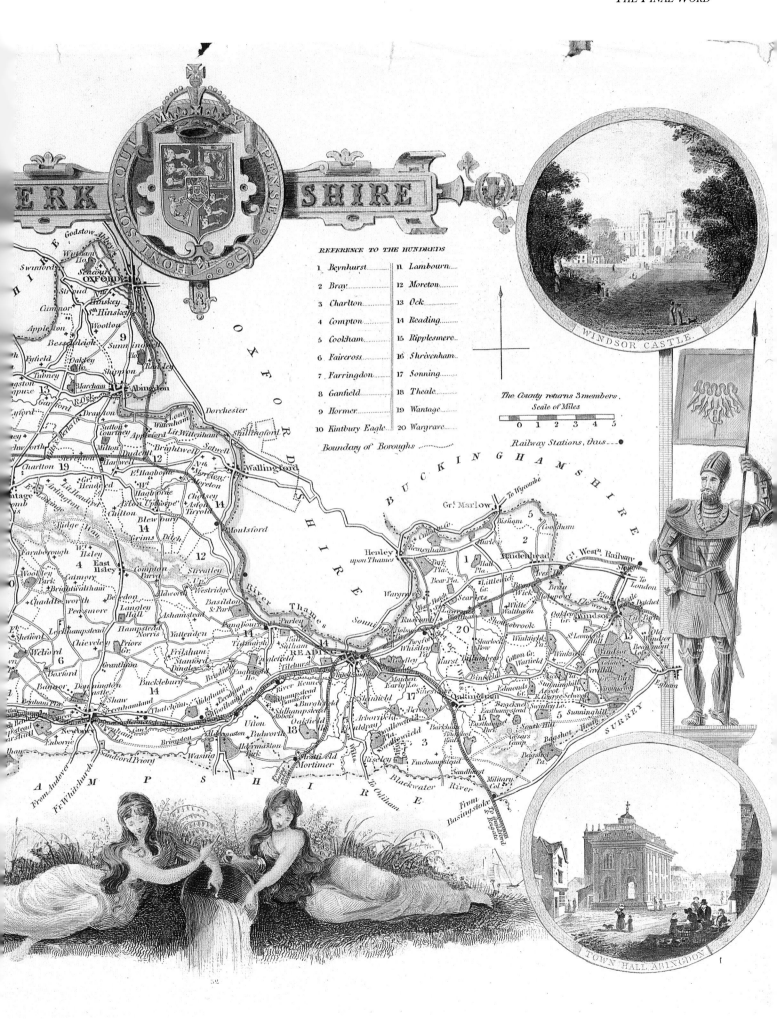

REFERENCE TO THE HUNDREDS

1	Beynhurst	11	Lambourn
2	Bray	12	Moreton
3	Charlton	13	Ock
4	Compton	14	Reading
5	Cookham	15	Ripplesmere
6	Faircross	16	Shrivenham
7	Farringdon	17	Sonning
8	Ganfield	18	Theale
9	Hormer	19	Wantage
10	Kintbury Eagle	20	Wargrave

Boundary of Boroughs ....

The County returns 3 members.
Scale of Miles
0 1 2 3 4 5

Railway Stations, thus ___•

WINDSOR CASTLE.

TOWN HALL ABINGDON

GLOSSARY

AIR
One of the four Elements. The Air Signs are Libra, Aquarius and Gemini.

ANGLES
Four extra-sensitive points on a birth chart: the Ascendant; the IC (*Imum Coeli*); the Descendant; and the MC (*Medium Coeli*, or Midheaven).
The Angles correspond to the First, Fourth, Seventh and Tenth Houses respectively.

AQUARIUS
The eleventh Sign of the Zodiac.

ARIES
The first Sign of the Zodiac.

ASCENDANT
The Sign and degree of the Zodiac which is rising over the eastern horizon at the time and place of birth.

ASPECT
The geometric angle between two or more Planets. Aspects can be harmonious and helpful, or challenging, according to the Planets involved and the number of degrees between them.

ASTROLOGY
From Greek, meaning 'star'. The study of the correlation of planetary configurations with events on Earth.

BENEFIC
Planets conferring a fortunate effect. Jupiter is known as the 'greater benefic', and Venus the 'lesser benefic'.

IRTH TIME
The moment when a child takes its first breath.

CANCER
The fourth Sign of the Zodiac.

CAPRICORN
The tenth Sign of the Zodiac.

CARDINAL SIGN
The Signs of Aries, Cancer, Libra and Capricorn. Cardinal Signs initiate action.

CONJUNCTION
A planetary aspect when two or more Planets occupy the same degree of the Zodiac, or are within eight degrees of one another.

CUSP
The dividing point, or line, between Signs or Houses.

DESCENDANT
The opposite point to the Ascendant, marking the cusp of the Seventh House.

EARTH
One of the four Elements. The Earth Signs are Capricorn, Taurus and Virgo.

ELEMENTS
Four divisions of ether: Fire, Earth, Air and Water. There are three Signs of the Zodiac assigned to each Element.

EQUINOX
The astronomical points marking the first day of Spring at 0 degrees Aries (the Vernal Equinox) and the first day of Autumn at 0 degrees Libra (the Autumnal Equinox). At these two points, day and night are of equal length.

FIRE
One of the four Elements. The Fire Signs are Aries, Leo and Sagittarius.

FIXED SIGNS
The Fixed Signs are Taurus, Leo, Scorpio and Aquarius. Fixed Signs stabilize.

GEMINI
The third Sign of the Zodiac.

GEOCENTRIC
Earth-centred. The view of the Solar System from Earth, from where it appears that the Sun, Moon and Planets orbit the Earth. Astrology is geocentric; astronomy is heliocentric, or Sun-centred.

HOROSCOPE
From Latin *hora* (time) and Greek *skopos*, (observer). An observation of the hour of birth. The terms 'Horoscope' and 'birth chart' are interchangeable.

HOUSES
Twelve, not necessarily equal, divisions of the
birth chart, beginning with the Ascendant, and
running anti-clockwise round the chart.

IC
The *Imum Coeli* (literally 'the undersky').
The lower meridian, and the opposite point of the MC.
It marks the cusp of the Fourth House.

LEO
The fifth Sign of the Zodiac.

LIBRA
The seventh Sign of the Zodiac.

MALEFIC
Planets conferring an unfortunate influence.
Saturn is known as the 'greater malefic', and Mars as
the 'lesser malefic'.

MUTABLE SIGNS
These are Gemini, Virgo, Sagittarius and Pisces.
Mutable Signs adapt.

NATAL CHART
A Horoscope, or birth chart

NATURAL CHART
A birth chart with Aries on the Ascendant.

NEGATIVE SIGNS
Water and Earth Signs

PISCES
The twelfth Sign of the Zodiac.

PLANET
From Greek *planetes* (wanderer). For astrological
convenience, the Sun and Moon are included as
Planets, together with Mercury, Venus, Mars, Jupiter,
Saturn, Uranus, Neptune and Pluto.

POSITIVE SIGNS
Fire and Air Signs.

RISING PLANET
A Planet situated within eight degrees of the
Ascendant.

RISING SIGN
The Sign of the Zodiac appearing on the eastern
horizon (the Ascendant) at the moment of birth.

RULING PLANET
The planetary ruler of the ascending Sign.

SAGITTARIUS
The ninth Sign of the Zodiac.

SCORPIO
The eighth Sign of the Zodiac.

SOLAR CHART
A birth chart where the position of the Sun
(its Zodiacal degree) is also used as the Ascendant
when the time of birth (and therefore the true
Ascendant) is unknown. All newspaper Sun Sign
columns are calculated in this way.

SOLSTICE
From Latin *sol* (the Sun), and *sistere* (to stand still). A
point when the Sun appears to stand still at the time of
its greatest northern or southern declination
(angular distance north or south of the Equator). The
Summer Solstice occurs at 0 degrees Cancer, and the
Winter Solstice at 0 degrees Capricorn. In southern
hemispheres, of course, the Solstices are reversed.

TAURUS
The second Sign of the Zodiac.

VIRGO
The sixth Sign of the Zodiac.

WATER
One of the four Elements. The Water Signs are Cancer,
Scorpio and Pisces.

ZODIAC
From Greek *zodiakos* (circle of animals). The Zodiac is
a band extending to eight degrees either side of the
Ecliptic (the apparent path of the Sun round the
Earth), on which the twelve Signs of the Zodiac are
disposed.

INDEX

ACKNOWLEDGEMENTS

Electric Ephemeris, 396 Caledonian Road, London N1 1DN kindly provided the birth charts and astrological data used in this book, together with invaluable advice and assistance, for which the author is extremely grateful.

The quotations from *Live Aid* and *Is That It?* are reproduced by kind permission of Sidgwick & Jackson Limited. Thanks are due to Eric Glass Ltd. for kind permission to quote from *The Unforgiving Minute*. Excerpts from the speeches of Sir Winston Churchill are reproduced by kind permission of Curtis Brown Ltd. on behalf of the estate of Sir Winston Churchill © Copyright: the estate of Sir Winston Churchill.

JILL DAVIES

The publishers would like to thank the following organizations and individuals for their kind permission to reproduce the photographs in this book.

Bridgeman Art Library: 8-9; 48-49 (Vatican Museums & Galleries); 86 (National Trust, Petworth House); 92 (Christopher Wood Gallery); 98 (Osterreichische Gallery); 119 (Thyssen-Bornemisza Collection); Bubbles: 42 (Lois Thurston); 72 (Julie Fisher); Camera Press: 105 (Philippe Halsman); Bruce Coleman Ltd: 118 (Carl Wallace); Zoe Dominic: 128-129; Mary Evans Picture Library: 96; 120; 126; 133; Ronald Grant Archive: 54; 56; 57 left; 67 bottom; 70; 73; 110; 121; Sally & Richard Greenhill: 106; Susan Griggs Agency: 134; Hulton-Deutsch Collection: 87; 111; 112-113; 118; 136; 148; Images Colour Library: 2; 10; Image Bank: 78; 112; 140; 148; Katz Pictures: 77; 96-97; 135 (SNAP); 78-79 (Jeff Slocombe/Outline); 129 (Tom Stoddart); 142-143 (Richard Baker); Kobal Collection: 52-53; 55; 90; 141; London Features International: 51 (Josh Tracei); 57 left (Colin Mason); 58 (Phil Loftus); 59 left (Bert Six); 63; 92; 92-93; 124-125 (Fran Griffin); 132-140 (Micelotta); 150; Magnum Photos Ltd: 134 (Sergio Larrain); Peter Newark's Pictures: 116; Octopus Picture Library: 151; Michael le Poer Trench: 153; Jonathan Potter: 154-155; Retna: 64 (Henry Diltz); 104 (Michael Putland); Rex Features Ltd: 57 right (Trippett); 59 right (Bravo Press); 60; 61; 62 (Dezzo Hoffman); 64-65 (Bill Gentile/Sipa Press); 66 (Pierre Villard); 67 top; 83; 84-85; 99 (Globe Photos Inc.); 144 (Eddie Boldizsar); 150 (George James/Globe Photos Inc.); 152 Science Photo Library: 6-7 (Jerry Schad) Tony Stone Worldwide: 84 (Jo Brown/Mick Smee); 106-107 (Jon Gray); 126 (Jeremy Walker); Topham Picture Source: 126-7; 145 (Associated Press); 149.

Illustrations by Tony Hannaford